A FAMILY GROUP, MOULMEIN (*p.* 68)

A BACHELOR GIRL
IN BURMA

BY

G. E. MITTON

AUTHOR OF "A BACHELOR GIRL IN LONDON"
"JANE AUSTEN AND HER TIMES," ETC.

CONTAINING NINETY-FIVE ILLUSTRATIONS
FROM PHOTOGRAPHS

LONDON

ADAM AND CHARLES BLACK

1907

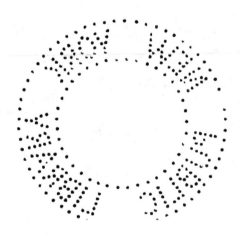

AUTHOR'S NOTE

In explanation of the title, I must state that bachelor girls are scarce in Burma. I was sitting one evening in the gymkhana club at Rangoon between two married ladies. We had all three been enlarging on the fascination of the land and the delights of being there, when one of them broke out abruptly, "How lucky you are! You travel about and see it all, and yet you are free. Mrs. R. and I *had to get* married to come here!"

This is one way of looking at it.

For another, *see* p. 55.

This is not a book "on Burma." The touching confidence of friends in my ability was shown by repeated queries as to whether I was going to "do" a book "on Burma" after I had been there two months. There is no doubt, of course, that I could have written a complete and exhaustive account of the people and the land, including all the wild tribes of the north, without knowing a single word of their languages—these things come so much by intuition—but I preferred to save the said friends the brain-work such a course would entail, so have written a book which cannot be said to be "on" anything unless it be "on the surface." I have put down what I saw and what I did, and fear that " I " is writ large over all the pages. I saw things and heard things and they amused me, I told them to others and they amused them, and so I have written them down on paper in the hope they may amuse even those I do not know personally. I have refrained from generalising on the basis of one example, and when a bit of history is absolutely necessary I have taken it straight from the pages of the best authority I know—with quotation marks.

The book, such as it is, owes its genesis entirely to the suggestion and encouragement of Mrs. Percival Marshall of Moulmein, without whose kindness and hospitality I could never have gone to Burma. It was also through her that I gained a little peep behind the scenes into the ways of the Burmese ladies in their everyday life; for many persons who have lived for years in Burma do not know a single Burman on social terms.

I have to mention also with warm gratitude the sympathetic help I received from the Lieutenant-Governor, Sir Herbert Thirkell White, K.C.I.E., and Lady Thirkell White, by whose kindness I was enabled to penetrate beyond the beaten tracks and to do much that would have been quite impossible otherwise.

As for the illustrations of the book, many friends have lent me photographs to supplement my own. I must acknowledge with thanks those of Mr. Sydney H. Reynolds, who is responsible for no fewer than twelve; that on p. 96 taken by Mr. J. MacGeorge, of Moulmein; that on p. 181 by Mrs. Bingham, and that on p. 193 by Captain J. H. Brunskill, R.A.M.C.

When not otherwise stated, the illustrations are, with one exception, from my own photos, taken by a No. 4 cartridge kodak. The results show how much may be done with a good camera even by a complete amateur.

G. E. MITTON.

CONTENTS

ILLUSTRATIONS

CHAPTER I

THE LAND OF PROMISE

WHENEVER for a moment the rushing stream of concentrated thought and action ceases and my mind drops into a backwater of idleness, the voices of those around me grow insignificant, the affairs they speak of pale in comparison with the pictures that arise clear and sharp before my mental vision.

Once again in the rapidly darkening day, while the sunset flashes luridly yellow, I steam past the towering crag in the middle defile of the Irrawaddy; the wash of the pent-in current swirls around the narrowed corner, the hoot of the syren sounds in my ears, and in response to that warning there spring out in the darkness the dropping fires of two torches held at arm's length by figures seemingly carved in bronze at the two extremes of a fifty-foot raft.

Or I am lying back on the verandah of the dâk bungalow at Bhamo, not far from the Chinese frontier, and see framed in dark teak a raised causeway lying across a plain bounded by blue hills, and along the causeway there comes a convoy of mules kicking up the dust; the tinkle of their bells rings in my ears over the prickly cactus plants and the scant herbage, while their

A

drivers, in enormous limpet hats and wide white trousers, run after them, at the beginning of a journey up into those hills and beyond, a journey that will last two months at least.

Or I look up at a steep cliff of clay and see at the summit the gorgeously dressed Palaungs, like huge red and blue parrots, silhouetted against a background of pinnacles and pagodas and palms and sunlight.

Or I pass in the spirit amid the courts of the great golden pagoda in Rangoon, and hear the monotonous chant of the worshippers as they bow themselves before a mighty brass image, that gleams out of a dim shrine by the light of a hundred tiny candles guttering on the ground. In the warm and dream-like dusk the smell of the incense is wafted to my nostrils, and the fragrance of the frangipanni perfumes the air like scent. I could go on with a hundred of such scenes, all different, and all indelibly impressed on my brain ; for the charm of the most fascinating country in the world, the country of Burma, has laid hold upon me and will be with me to the end.

It was the fulfilment of a dream that I should go there, in spite of the difficulty of getting away long enough to cross to the other side of the world, in spite of such sordid considerations as money, in spite of the effort required to break away from daily routine. Burma combines so much : the glory of the East ; the mystery of the unknown, in its strange tribes and races as yet but half understood, even by those who have studied them most ; the fascination of nature untamed ; and the comfort of travelling under British rule. The charm of this most fascinating land lies not in its beauty, for beauty Ceylon can beat it easily, but in its variety. Ceylon with her rich jungle-covered hills and her glorious vistas cannot call one back as does Burma of the flat paddy-fields, of the pariah dogs and the dusty villages.

As a holiday-land Burma is only just beginning to be known ; while Egypt has attracted its thousands Burma has as yet only had its tens, the bloom of it is untouched, its ways are as yet uncrowded. Yet this is bound to be altered in a year or two, for the trip is after all extraordinarily cheap. The return fare for two years by one of the Bibby boats, the principal line direct to Burma, is only £75. No expensive wardrobe is required, and away from the one or two large towns, where it must be confessed the hotel charges are exorbitant, there are dâk bungalows put up by Government for the use of travellers, to be occupied at the reasonable rate of one rupee four annas (1s. 8d.) a night. To this certain small charges for " sweeper," etc., are added, and the food can be arranged with the derwan or keeper for four rupees eight annas a day (6s.), or if one is staying more than a day or two in one place it comes cheaper still to let one's own native " boy " do the catering and cooking.

A native boy is indispensable to any one going about the country who knows neither Hindustanee nor Burmese. For about thirty rupees a month, or possibly twenty-five, with an added four annas a day " butter-money," a boy can be easily engaged, but the worst of it is that many of them are very unsatisfactory. They are almost invariably Madrassees or other natives of India, and are as a rule good linguists, but are very ready to

take advantage of the slightest weakness in their master
or mistress for their own purposes.   I was told by those
who had had much experience in the matter that nine
out of ten are untrustworthy, but the tenth, when you
can get him, is a treasure, who will faithfully serve
you.

The time to make the trip is in the beginning of
November and the time to return is March, as after
that the hot weather comes to make existence in a
tropical climate wearisome to the flesh.   I started on
November 8, joining the *Cheshire*, Bibby line, at
Birkenhead, and going right round with her instead of
overland to Marseilles as many passengers do.

When we were fairly started and out of the Mersey
it was very rough indeed, so rough the Bibby pilot had
to stay on board and go to Marseilles with the boat
instead of being put ashore at Holyhead as usual.
During the night I heard tons of water thundering
down on the decks and rushing out of the scuppers with
a wash and gurgle.   About four in the morning, while
I was being pitched from side to side in my bunk, I
was startled by the crash of some heavy object coming
bang up against the wall of the cabin at every lurch;
the steward when summoned searched in vain some time
for the cause, but at last discovered a wheel-barrow
which had been left at large in the coal-bunkers below!

I was lucky enough to escape sea-sickness, though for
the next two days I preferred to have my meals on
deck rather than go into the saloon.   At last, however,
when Captain Langston good-humouredly remarked on
the very un-invalidish plates of roast lamb I and a fellow

passenger were consuming with enjoyment, we thought it about time to make the effort and begin meals indoors.

The *Cheshire* and the *Shropshire,* twin-steamers, are the smallest now in the Bibby fleet, and I had opportunities for comparing them, for I came home in the *Shropshire.* I also spent the four days between Rangoon and Colombo on the *Herefordshire,* one of the largest boats on this line, but I preferred the smaller ones. On all Bibby liners only first-class passengers are carried ; this not only gives them the run of the whole ship, including the use of the lower decks as skittle-decks, but makes a very homely feeling on board. The difference between these boats and some of the great floating palaces, of many decks and many classes, is best expressed by saying it is comparable with the difference between staying at your own club and at an hotel.

It may not be generally known that every officer in the Bibby fleet must hold a master's certificate, and in that respect at least is equal to the captain, a fact which should inspire the passengers with a feeling of security.

A long sea voyage on a passenger steamer is like nothing else ; the ship is a world in itself ; other people, other interests, other anxieties drop from one, the petty excitements and games on board loom large in importance. Some voyages are from the beginning dull, the passengers break into sets and one set refuses to know another ; there are jealousies and coolnesses, but all who were there agreed in saying that there never had been such a pleasant voyage as the one I was lucky enough to experience as my first.

The relations of passengers to each other would

furnish forth a book in itself. Lives there a person who does not think that he or she is entitled to a three-berth cabin to himself or herself while others may be crammed three together? Lives there any one who does not resent the advent of new passengers, who cause a little more discomfort, as if they were a source of personal injury, and had no right to come on board at all? These feelings there were no doubt on the *Cheshire*, they are indigenous to human nature, but they were kept in check by the atmosphere of general good-humour and friendliness. The types on board ship would furnish forth much delightful material for any one who could appreciate them. There is the lady who will be first, but who, if she is allowed that premier position, is a real acquisition, for she is a born leader, and can organise with spirit and originality; there is the hoyden, whose loud laugh and too exuberant manners are always bringing her under the displeasure of her married sister, the sister who is comfortably established in the East, and is kindly taking her out to secure a like advantage ; there is the spoilt child, who inspires every one on board, except his parents, with a frantic desire to administer a spanking; there is the stuffy man, wholly out of place on a ship, who keeps his port-hole hermetically sealed, to the disgust and suffering of his cabin companions, and who complains of draughts in the Red Sea ; there is the old maiden lady, never seen without her knitting, who has plain features, and looks sharp and sour, but is in reality one of the shrewdest and kindest-hearted people on board. My fellow travellers may fit the caps here offered, and are at perfect liberty to wear them if they choose, but I can assure them they are not "made to measure"!

To those who are quite novices there is a great deal that is interesting on the ship itself: the crew of Lascars with their weather-stained blue uniforms and shining eyes; the mystery of the engines; the working of the great ship: the extreme point of the fo'castle head, where there is nothing between you and the great ocean, and you may feel you are riding forward into space; the weird noises at nights, the rattles and groans and creaks, and every now and then the monotonous chant from the crow's-nest, when at the hour, after the bells have sounded, the two Lascars on the look-out cry in their own tongue: Ham dekte hain (I am looking out); Bati ackha Sahib (The lamps are burning brightly).

The voyage itself is of course much more interesting than that over the Atlantic or to South America, where little or no land can be seen all the way; there is perpetual variety, though there are few stoppages.

The first land we saw was Cape St. Vincent, and thereafter, at the unearthly hour of 5.30 A.M.. we were warned that we were passing Gibraltar; the old hands only snuggled down afresh, but the novices, among whom I was one, tried to struggle up on deck. I put on my big fur coat and a scarf over my head, and reeled up the companion way overcome by sleep, but I woke soon enough when I reached the deck, for a blast of bitter wind drove around, and I stepped into a flood of water where the men were washing the decks. I struggled up higher and came out on the saloon deck only to find it

exposed and soaking; it was raining and blowing at the
same time.   Another woe-begone shadow inquired of
me where was Gibraltar, but I could not answer, for the
view around was as black as night.   Together we made
for a sheltered corner under an awning and leaning over
the rail excitedly demonstrated to each other by signs
that " Gib " must be where the great moon-like light-
house blinked and went out every few seconds.   As we
were thus engaged a wild shower of sparks swept down
upon us from the bridge, where they were setting off
rockets in signal.   Between fire and water we had a
lively time of it; but we hung on until, as the faintest
signs of dawn appeared, we did actually see something
of the mighty rock, towering far higher than we had
anticipated.   However, to make up, we spent radiant
hours the next day lazily watching the sierras of Spain
as we passed along the coast.   Great hills rising into
misty clouds, with slopes and ravines and gullies glowing
with colour, purple and blue and green and grey; I have
never looked upon any scenery which could so fitly be
described as opal, for there were even flashes of a kind of
ruddy tinge here and there.   In the crinkles were little
white villages, with the houses falling away in straggling
lines adown the slopes, and here and there a tiny white-
walled enclosure denoting a graveyard.

Marseilles is as well known to English people as Dover,
but to our insatiable eagerness it was full of interest.
We went up the funicular railway to the Church of
Notre Dame de la Garde, crowned by the massive gilded
figure of the Virgin, which looks down on a panorama
of sea and shore, and sharp ranges of white rock out-

lined by masses of dark foliage. Rocky islets stud the
sea, and on one stands " Monte Cristo's " Castle, easily
to be mistaken for the rock which forms its foundation.
After Marseilles the next great excitement was passing
Stromboli, which also occurred in the dark chilly hours
of the morning—they did not arrange these things well
for our comfort. It was so dark when we arrived on
deck that we could not see the conical peak uprising from
the sea at all, but as the sun rose, and the sky swept from
pale primrose and apple to orange, it came up black
against it, and in the midst of the blackness there burst
out a great puff of flame, and the lava ran down the side
like burning coals. The quicksilver sea meantime
turned to electric blue, the tiny white houses smiled out
at us from the lower slopes, and we suddenly awoke
from our absorption to find that the garments in which
we had come out lightly attired were hardly suitable for
the full whiteness of day.

On a Sunday morning we passed through the Straits
of Messina, and saw the shining cone of Etna glowing
silver with snow, dominating all the scene. Fascinating
villages clustered along the shore ; one of them built
into and upon a mighty mass of rock, stupendous in
size, and looking from the ship exactly like a giant's castle.

We arrived at Port Said on November 21, and were
immediately surrounded by a flotilla of boats thronged
with men of every colour and in every costume. The
hybrid English, cosmopolitan slang, and native impudence
make up an impressive whole. In its goods for sale, as
in other things, Port Said borrows from all nations, and
the lace, trinkets, enamel, and silver work which are

B

offered are all offered at the hands of the middleman. My impressions of the place are of dirt, dust, tawdriness, extreme good-humour and a liberal overflow of officiousness. Every man in the main street has nothing better to do than to escort the newly landed from one shop to another, hoping that if he is lucky he will get " backsheesh " from the victim and more from his fleecer in the shop. However, in spite of all, it is worth going ashore even though on return you have the sensation of having escaped from a swarm of blue-bottles which has been buzzing persistently around you.

In the evening the tawdriness vanishes, the lights gleam golden, red or green; they shine on the still water ; and the canal offices, with their little sea-green domes, rise against the lurid sky ; innumerable boats crawl around like glow-worms, and the babel resolves itself into a subdued and distant murmur. Then comes the canal ! Among other and richer memories this still holds its own, because of the quality of mystery which entered into it.

When we had fairly started, the steamer crept on so silently and slowly, that except for the ripple on the viscid water one could not have known she was moving. On each side were dim sandbanks dotted by white posts and diversified by dark shadows. The mystery of the night deepened. In the west, low down, a half-moon, lying horizontally, dropped almost perceptibly. On the same side, above and beyond the sandbank, was a vast lake of shimmering water, and as the moon fell towards its surface her reflection broadened and became a wide pathway of orange light. Lower she fell, and deeper grew her dusky tinge in the mirk, until she seemed not so much a moon as some solid three-sided object projected on an infinitely distant sky.

The lights for a signal shone out ahead—two whites and a red—which, being interpreted, means: " Draw up at the next siding." On arrival there we found two cargo boats already tethered, and we took up a station behind them. In the interval of stillness that followed we had time to notice the faint hiss of escaping steam, the shimmering of stars in the oily water; Orion and Sirius rising higher than ever seen in England ; then far ahead shone out a brilliant coruscating light, shooting a thousand jewelled rays along the water. There was so much grandeur in the noiseless approach of this apparently unsupported light, that even the chatter on the saloon deck fell into silence. On it came, and as its direct rays ran past our eyes and ceased to blind us, we saw behind it the towering bows and high decks of a French battleship. Her portholes, crowded by eager faces, her barbettes, her guns, and her warlike apparatus slipped before us and vanished ; another came and yet another. It was close on midnight, and still they came, altogether eight ships, four of them battleships, and as each one receded from us, in slow majesty, the lights of the next striking on her through the miasmic mist, now rising from the water, transformed her into a phantom ship seen in a fiery blue glow. The searchlights upon the water attracted a multitude of small wriggling fish, which leaped and squirmed, alive with phosphorus, until one had to rub one's eyes to believe their record true.

So much for the canal by night.

By day the desert is seen, and the magic of it lies in the fact that it is so exactly what a desert should be. The pinky-yellow sand, the lines of purple haze, the ridge of barren hills, the tufted palms and little oases, the peasants working in the sun, the donkeys grazing, the camps where camels lie and chew the cud in haughty unconcern, and by the side of the canal the little station houses apparently cut out of yellow cardboard, all this is just what one expects to see.

Both going and returning the sea at Suez was of an overpowering blueness, a blueness such as I never saw matched even in the Far East, ranging all the way from turquoise to prussian and infinitely varied; for this alone Suez may be remembered.

It was after Suez that we first tried sleeping out on deck. I had seen the notice that the upper deck was reserved for ladies at night, when I boarded the steamer at Tilbury, to get a look at her before she went round to Liverpool, and imagination had transported me from the grey lowering skies and dirty atmosphere of the docks straightway to a picture of tropical calm, a moon-lit ship upon a moonlit sea, where she made hardly any motion as she floated beneath a gorgeous tropical sky studded with stars. The reality was different. The steward being apprised of the intention of several ladies to take advantage of the deck accommodation rolled up bed and bedding in huge sausages with a practised hand, and we, trembling at the upward flight through the still lighted passages in scanty bed attire, fled after him. The lights were out in the drawing-room through which we had to pass, and from the

blackness of the floor various voices piteously wailed,
" Oh, take care, that's my head ! "   " Don't tread on
me ! " " Here I am, can't you see ? "   Stepping gingerly
I arrived on the warm smooth deck, which however was
so completely covered with awnings that only at one
side could we get glimpses of any stars.   Peering down
over the rail I saw the sheeted foam racing past, with
here and there the bright starlike phosphorescence out-
shining the moonlight.   Dim figures joined me, and a
wild skirt dance was executed before we peered down
to read our names written in chalk on the deck beside
our respective bedding.   There was a good deal of
wind, and altogether it was not much like being cradled
in the tropic calm I had foreseen.   It was difficult to
get into bed at all when the wind wrenched sheets and
blankets and threw them playfully aside ; dressing-
gowns and bed-shoes had to be carefully tucked under
the mattresses or they would have gone overboard.
Then to sleep while the steady tramp of the officer on
the bridge overhead sounded to and fro, and every half-
hour the din of the bells clanged right in our ears.
Soon after eight bells (midnight) a short oblivion
visited my sleepy eyes to be ended abruptly in a wild
start when I awoke to pandemonium ! Everything
seemed to be shrieking and screaming and whistling at
once, the awnings snapped like pistol-shots, the wind
yelled, the sails groaned and strained, the air was full
of salt, and my face and hands were stinging intolerably.
with it.   I wondered if I could, if I dare, make a dash
for the shelter of the drawing-room.   But there was so
much to get hold of, slippers, pillows, bed-clothes and

dressing-gown, and to let one go would be to part from it for good. I simply clung on with hands and nails in desperation, and after a while dozed again. Yet when six bells (4 A.M.) rang out the wind was blowing worse, so I made one effort, grabbed everything into an armful, and leaving the mattress alone, to stick to the deck if it could, collapsed in a corner of the drawing-room on to a heap of cushions and soon slept again.

Besides the wind, another drawback to sleeping on deck was the early awakening. At 5 A.M. the electric lights were turned on from the bridge, and she would be a hardy sleeper indeed who could withstand their glare; one had to rise and stumble downstairs with bedding all in a heap, for the Lascars were waiting to swab the decks.

We had, of course, all the usual board-ship amusements, the fancy dress ball, the book dinner, the gymkhana, and skittle competitions, and we had some that were not usual. One extraordinary hoax took in nearly every one on board. Somewhere in the Red Sea, one of the wits among the men started the idea of getting up a football match with a Colombo team on arrival. The suggestion was received enthusiastically; every morning in the early hours a string of bare-footed pyjama-clad men raced round the decks training. At Perim a wire was supposed to have been sent ashore requesting the Colombo team to be in readiness. The whole affair was kept up with great spirit until the last morning before we arrived at Colombo, when printed slips containing a full account of the great match, describing how one player had "sprained his wind," and

" Hackenschmidt, Ceylon's renowned full-back " distin-
guished himself, were distributed, and the mighty joke,
which had deceived all but the initiators, and lasted
a full fortnight, was " blown " amid roars of laughter.

The first paper ever printed on board a Bibby boat
was published this voyage ; the last thing in it was by
no means the least clever :

> He thought he saw a battered hat
> That danced the Highland fling ;
> He looked again and saw it was
>   A football match in swing.
> " Tis clear," said he, " when we go East
>   Things get more interesting ! "

CHAPTER II

THE SPICY-SMELLING EAST

THE night before the steamer arrived at Colombo there was a pervading sadness on board; those who had been the wildest among the younger set of men going out for the first time, fell into melancholy as suddenly as does a puppy who has bumped himself in the midst of an uproarious game. There was a great golden moon too, which intensified the melancholy, and it was hardly to be wondered at that some leant over the railings and gazed into the depths, without answering when they were spoken to. So long as they were on board all these young fellows, these prospective tea-planters and engineers, had been among friends; they were not severed from England, and the life on board was a holiday, an interregnum, which might legitimately be enjoyed, but now they were to launch off into a new and untried life, from whence they could not return for many years, a life where success or failure awaited them, and in which their powers and attainments were to become real weapons in the carving out of a career.

Yet in the morning, when Colombo was seen rising behind her lovely bay of blue and green dancing water, these thoughts were dissipated as a mist before a tropical sun, and all was life and energy and high spirits once more.

One's first sight of the East; can it ever be forgotten? Countless books and colour illustrations and other people's descriptions have made it familiar, but the real sight comes as a surprise, one awakes suddenly from a dream and finds it true. The first excitement was the arrival of the " husbands' boat," bringing the men who had been separated from their wives for months, or even years. It was extremely interesting, for I had grown so intimate with many of the wives that I could not help having speculations upon the individuality and appearance of the husbands. It was a trying time for both, poor things, for the launch could not come up to the gangway at once, but was kept knocking up and down on the choppy waves near by, while sun-reddened faces, crowned by topees, peered up from under the awning at the steamer's deck high above, where stood the excited women. Cries of " There he is, there's daddy, see dear, oh no it isn't!"

" Can't you see him?" " What, that one? Oh yes, so it is!" echoed around on all sides.

Children grown from toddling babes to boys and girls were ready to shout " daddy" to any sunburnt stranger, and the buzz of excitement amongst their mothers was tempered by a quite perceptible nervousness.

Then came the rush up the gangway, the variety of greetings, ranging from the warm hug to the formal nod. It was very funny to see how mindful of convention were some, how totally regardless of onlookers others.

c

Not long after came our turn to go ashore, and as we set foot on the dark shady wharf the whiff of the "spicy" smell came to our nostrils, and we felt we really were in the East. It is better to see Colombo before Rangoon, for Colombo fulfils all one's expectations, Rangoon woefully disappoints them. The cleanness of Colombo, the smooth broad red roads, the rickshaws, the emerald-green foliage, are all elements of delight, and then the drive along the Galle Face parade, with the mother-of-pearl waves breaking in creamy surf, and the palms waving around the hotel ahead, is purely entrancing. The Galle Face is one of the finest hotels in the world, the wind blows ever through its lofty halls and open corridors, and rustles the leaves of the great growing plants. One steps straight from the arcade to a smooth green terrace running right down to the beach, and in the evening the palms are decorated with countless electric lights set amid the foliage and gleaming like rubies and sapphires. To stand here in the warm scented dusk and listen to the breaking of the surf at one's feet is an experience never to be forgotten.

It was tea-time when we arrived, and we were all glad enough to get a real cup of tea after a long course of ship's tea and condensed milk, and afterwards we went, a party of five, for a drive in rickshaws to the Botanical Gardens. The trees were gorgeous with flowers, some dropping fire in flaming bunches, some lit up by large yellow blossoms like gloxinias, and others covered with a mass of mauve. The only thing that jarred the feelings was the sight of the poor miserable wild beasts kept in a torturing captivity in cages ridiculously inadequate.

Coming back the night fell with startling suddenness. One minute we saw a silver-blue lake against a mass of black foliage outlined on a saffron sky, and the next it was gone and all was dark.

The first night on Eastern soil is strange in many ways : the mosquito nets, the little lizards running about the distempered walls, the squawk of the menacing crows at the window, all remind one strongly that one is not in England. I left early the next morning to rejoin the ship, leaving many dear friends behind in this land of delight ; I felt the parting with two particularly, but we agreed to meet again ; either I was to return to them and spend some time in Ceylon on the way home, or they would come over and join me in Burma.

The next few days to Rangoon were sad : half the passengers had disembarked, life had gone out of everything. The porpoises were still with us and the flying-fish, we could still go to the fo'castle head, and watch the great frill of foam falling away each side from the cutting bows, but these things depend so much for their interest on the companions who share them with you ! It was not until sunrise on December 8, when, aroused by an unexpected noise, I sleepily peered out of my porthole and saw the pilot leap aboard high over the bulwarks outlined against a sky of orange and red, that I revived. We were at the mouth of the river then, and the water was French grey and very smooth ; when we were still afar off, churning up the mud between the flat

spongy banks, we saw the gleam of *the* Pagoda, and felt
that after all what we had gone through was but a
prelude to the real thing—here was Burma!

It is astonishing that Pagoda! From a distance it
appears high as if it stood on a hill dominating the
town, as one gets nearer it drops down and becomes in-
conspicuous, but when one comes really near, it rises
again, and is found to be on a majestic ridge.

I had very little idea what I was going to do on
arrival; the friend, Mrs. M., who had persuaded me to
come out to Burma, lived at Moulmein, which is a day's
journey across the bay from Rangoon, and I did not
know whether she intended to meet me or not; any way
I expected some sort of instructions to be awaiting me,
and did not worry myself at all. I was right to take
things quietly, for I found my welfare had been very
abundantly provided for; before any one else went
ashore the Government House launch was alongside,
and an A.D.C. who came in it carried me off to enjoy
the hospitality of the first lady in the land at Government House, where I heard that Mrs. M. was already
staying.

The glimpse I had of Rangoon as we rattled through
behind two fine horses was unsatisfactory. The place
lacks the colour and cleanness of Colombo; it is untidy,
unfinished, a town in the making. There are great
imposing stone buildings it is true, but they are set
amid small mean hovels and waste places covered with
lumber. The crowd is cosmopolitan, not by any means
distinctively Burman, and the general effect is bewildering. Then we passed into the broad well-kept roads

A CHUPRASSIE OUTSIDE GOVERNMENT
HOUSE, RANGOON

A CORNER IN THE SHWE DAGÓN PAGODA (*p.* 33)

running through Cantonments, as the European quarter is called, the residential part of Rangoon. Pleasant bungalows stood about in the midst of bare burnt brown lawns, but here and there were glorious masses of flaming poinsettia, and great bushes of royal purple bougainvillea.

Government House itself is a perfect palace, not beautiful externally, for it is built of yellow and red brick and terra cotta, but very fine within. On the steps was an imposing array of white clad chuprassies, with daggers in their belts, from which hung red tassels. I was most warmly and hospitably received by my charming hostess, whom I had already met in London, and affectionately greeted by Mrs. M., so soon felt at home.

In Government House everything has been designed to give space and air. The hall runs right up to a dome, and the upper stories are carried round it in a series of white arcades. The handsomely carved teak staircase is in two branches, passing up two sides. The floor is of mosaic, and a high arch opposite the entrance shows a glimpse of one of the most magnificent ball-rooms in the world. In spite of its airiness and spaciousness the hall is not bare, for it is decorated with fine specimens of Burmese wood-carving on a scale proportionate to its size ; two enormous elephant tusks are on the walls, and, as I saw it, there were almost always cannas, a kind of red and orange flag, a gallant flower, standing up in large vases and giving a dash of vivid colour. The downstairs servants are mostly Burmans, and wear turbans and lyungis of the purest purple, with snowy white engies or jackets.   One great charm of the native servant is the noiselessness of his approach, his bare feet make no sound on the floor.

I shall never forget my first awakening in this new land.   It was about 4 A.M. when I got out of bed and leaned from the high window.   The moon was still up, shedding a brilliant white light that made the shadows of the thick-foliaged trees dotting the lawns black by contrast.   The flat lawns, in spite of careful nightly watering, were not very green.   The smell of Burma came strongly to my nostrils, a smell I never afterwards could forget.   It is not so spicy as that of Ceylon, but rather a thin acrid smell as of something burnt, and to me it will for ever hereafter mean Burma.

The morning that followed was glorious ; it was like the fulness of a perfect midsummer day in England. The lawns were drenched with dew in the shade, but the yellow sunlight had quickly dried up all that came under its influence.   Chota hazri, consisting of tea and toast and bananas, here called plantains, was brought at 7.80, and breakfast downstairs followed at 9.80.   Between these hours the members of the household enjoyed their daily ride, for later the tremendous power of the sun made itself felt too strongly for enjoyment.   During the week I stayed here I saw the society side of Anglo-Burman life.   I was driven round the great lakes in Dalhousie Park, I was taken to hear the band at the Gymkhana Club, I visited Rangoon races, and attended various other entertainments.   Everything was so strange that I felt hopelessly bewildered and bemused.   The various races of natives in the streets were legion ; the language, or rather languages, for Hindustanee is as much spoken as Burmese, were so difficult; every detail, even down to the beetles in one's bath, was so unfamiliar, that it was quite a relief to catch sight of birds resembling English starlings and wagtails hopping about on the lawn! I was panting to know and find out something about the people and the land, but did not know where to begin. As a tentative step, when we were sitting in the great airy hall after breakfast, fanned by electric " punkahs," I expressed a desire to take a gharry and go down to the shops in the town. The ticca or hired gharries have one merit, that of being cheap, it is all you can say for them; you pay 12 annas the first hour and eight the next for a second-class one, and a little more for a first-class specimen. The body of the vehicle is built on the lines of a box or dog-kennel, and is so small that two Europeans can with difficulty sit there together, though six or eight Burmans frequently get in easily; the difference is not so much one of bulk as of temperament. The noise made by the iron-tyred wheels is so jarring that you feel inclined to stop your ears all the time. This of course does not affect the Burman, except agreeably; he likes any sort of noise rather than none. The windows or openings are provided with sun-shutters, often very necessary, but even when they are open you cannot see anything out of them but the road, unless you sit very low down with your feet up on the opposite seat to brace yourself from falling off.

My first raid on the town was a triumph of incompetency. My friend lent me her " butler," whom she had brought over with her. He was a Telugu, spoke English fluently, and seemed smart, but suffered from the worst defect of the native—glib superficiality. I was entirely dependent on him, as the gharry wallahs do not speak a word of English. They really require to be driven themselves by word of mouth, for it is very little use telling them where to go unless it is a well-known place, such as the station or principal hotel. They do not care to know their destination ; it is best to shout " right " or " left " at the turns, but as I did not then even know the Hindustanee for right and left, it was not much use trying this plan. Nearly all the low-class work in Burma down country, the work of coolies, gharry wallahs, etc., is done by the natives of India, who have swarmed over in their thousands. The Burmans consider these posts beneath their dignity, and it is unusual even to find Burman servants in private houses. Up-country the native is not quite so ubiquitous, and the coolie work of loading and unloading cargo from the steamers is almost wholly in Burman hands, that is to say, at present, for the native will no doubt arrive there also without any long delay. At first I could not understand that the word "native" invariably referred to the Indian native, and not the native of the land ; this is rather perplexing to a new comer.

My gharry wallah was a dark-skinned man with yellowish wrappings and turban ; he settled down on his box with his bare brown legs full in my view through the front opening of the gharry. The little rat-tailed pony seemed excessively far away, but this did not deter him from putting his heart into the business, and we

NUN AND MONK AT THE
SHWE DAGÔN PAGODA

AN IMAGE OF THE BUDDHA

started off at a tremendous pace. I had taken the precaution of getting a list of likely shops for what I wanted to buy from the A.D.C., and as we neared the town, which lay about two miles off, I called my escort, who was hanging on behind, on the little stand which always makes a convenient resting-place for the native servant, and asked him if he knew a certain shop.

"Yes, Missie, very good, Missie, very good," he replied. He sprang up again, and away we rattled once more. We pulled up in one of the principal streets, the man hopped down with alacrity and flung open the door with a flourish. I looked in vain for any sign of the shop I had come to seek.

"Is this it?" I asked doubtfully. "I don't see it. It is somewhere near the Strand hotel."

"Very good, Missie, very good," retorted my hench-man, eagerly slamming the door, and off we went again. This time we pulled up actually at the Strand hotel itself. I now began to understand that I was leaning on a broken reed, and that if I wanted anything doing I must do it myself. So I asked directions at the hotel and finding out what street the required shop was in I set the concern off in the right direction, and keeping a sharp look-out, shouted out to the driver to stop when I caught sight of the shop, then with a little panto-mimic waving and gesticulation I manœuvred him up to the right door. This business was more exciting than it sounds, for the shops stand back a considerable way from the streets in some places, the names are extremely irregular, and you have to watch both sides of the street at once. I grew quite hot with all this

exertion.   The next time I mentioned a shop I asked
my attendant if he really did know it, and this called
forth such profuse assurances that I was gullible
enough to believe him, especially as I had been told he
knew Rangoon.

I had asked for Orr and I arrived at Rowe!   I
thought at first that this was native inability to dis-
tinguish between OR and RO, but I have since come
to the conclusion that it was nothing so subtle, but
merely that the man being totally ignorant of the shop
I wanted, and quite incapable of confessing himself to
be so, took me to Rowe at a venture, that place being a
large general emporium much frequented by Europeans.
However, between these points I had seen several of
the other names on my list, so I did manage to compass
most of my shopping, but what with the unaccustomed
heat, the dust and the glare, I was nearly tired out
when I returned home.   After lunch, which was at two,
I was glad enough to retire to the palatial room, with
dressing-room and two bath-rooms attached, which I
shared with my friend Mrs. M.   I took the hot and
cold water taps and English baths for granted at
this time.   I had yet to learn the ways of the ordinary
bungalow.   It certainly was very hot, and every one
kept telling me what astonishingly hot "cold weather"
they were having, but I am one of those lucky mortals
whom a change of temperature does not greatly affect.
Of course I was grateful for the punkahs, and ice, and
midday siesta, without which the heat would have been
unbearable, but with these alleviations I felt ordinarily
quite well and active.   We had tea on the lawn, over

which the shadows of the trees had fallen, and this was always one of the most enjoyable times of the day; the sky still shone electric blue, but the sun had lost its deadly power. Alas, the interval for enjoyment was short, for darkness fell immediately after sunset. Many evenings we drove between tea and dinner, sometimes round the lakes in the park where the golden pagoda could be seen reflected in the water, then we stopped at Gossip Point, where nearly the whole of Rangoon was assembled in all descriptions of wheeled vehicles; and afterwards in the scented darkness, with the fireflies flashing around like diamonds, we went on to the Gymkhana Club. One day I was taken further afield to what are called the Big Lakes. The roads were smothered in red dust, and the great bullock-carts were a perpetual nuisance. The bullocks are yoked so wide apart that they walk in the ruts, and with their swelling sides occupy almost all the available road. In out-of-the-way districts such as I visited later I found out the reason for this. The roads there are often so heavily cut up that the centre is a mere hump almost grazing the axle of the cart. For any bullocks to keep a footing on it would be impossible, but when they walk in the deep broad ruts the cart scrapes along with comparative ease; the manner of yoking is therefore a survival of days when "made" roads of hard surface there were none.

On this drive we passed through a suburb of Rangoon called Kokine, and saw a native village of mat and mud houses and clinging smells, and came out at last by a rough field-road at one corner of a mighty lake heavily set with large islands. There was an orange light in the setting sun peculiar to Burma, a colour so rich and deep that it makes one feel one has never seen orange before.   The still foliage rose indigo and black against it, and in the clear air there came to our ears the howls of far-away pariah dogs and the squeaking of ungreased carts, which at a distance sounds like a confused murmur of talking voices.

But of all the sights of Rangoon none can come near the marvellous pagoda.   Other pagodas there are also, and the Sule or Soolay pagoda in the town might attract attention anywhere else ; but the Shwe Dagòn (pronounced Shway Dagone) is *the* pagoda above all in Burma.   It is seen in many aspects from many points of view.   It is always peeping at you, and you can never, while in Rangoon, lose the consciousness of its existence.

Then comes your first real introduction to it, and thenceforward it draws you again and again to see it under every aspect, under the garish light of day, under the mellow light of evening, and under the pure light of the moon, and every time you see it you think you have never seen it before and that you never can see it again, for that aspect which has just impressed itself upon you is the most perfect of all.   It touches you as if it were a living thing, for it seems as if all the petitions and adoration and cries of sorrowing humanity which have risen up around it for so many centuries have impregnated the mighty spire, and given it indeed in some sense the quality of life.

I had pictured it smooth and clean with a row of even roofs rising up to it in steps, but it is all uneven and heterogeneous.

The long ridge on which it stands is covered with trees from amid which the central pagoda or tope rises, and down one side and another run rows of more or less carved roofs enclosing the ascents. The most generally used of these and the finest is that on the south, and here I, in charge of one of the staff, was dropped one evening soon after my arrival.

The first porch or entry is new and tawdry, built in 1903; on each side are leogryphs of immense size. Then one reaches the older entrance, now partially hidden, and passes on up a long slippery cement slope, here and there broken by steps, and lined by stalls laden with sweetmeats, flowers, cigars, paper flags, and many other things, all of the flimsiest nature. At the moat there is an opening and a glimpse of the surrounding country, and then the way mounts steeply by numerous steps, between columns painted white and deeply stained at the bases by betel-nut ejections.

The fame of the Shwe Dagôn is a magnet which attracts Buddhists from all lands. Its special sanctity is because it contains such precious relics, viz. :

" Of the four human Buddhas of the present dispensation : the drinking-cup of Kawkathan, the robe of Gawnagong, the staff of Kathapa, and eight hairs of Gautama. Another version gives the staff of the first, the water-filter of the second, and a portion of the robe of the third, but, since they are absolutely inaccessible, the precise ownership is of the less importance. After the annexation a passage was cut from the niche facing the east entrance to the centre of the pagoda, which showed that the original pagoda has had seven casings added to it. The hti (the umbrella at the top) was thrown down by an earthquake in 1888, and a new one, valued at six lakhs, was put up by public subscription and with gratuitous labour. For many years the Shwe Dagôn was merely gilt and re-gilt. Since the beginning of the twentieth century it has been covered with thin gold plates as far up as the top of the inverted begging-bowl, whence the columnar spire rises through the 'twisted turban,' the 'lotos flower,' and the 'plantain-bud.' . . . Rangoon for every one except those who make their living there is the city of the Shwe Dagôn."*

At length, after a breathless ascent, we came out on to the platform. Directly opposite was a shrine resting at the base of the pagoda, and there are others, somewhat similar, at the four sides of the platform. In the centre rises the mighty gold pagoda bordered, between the larger shrines, by smaller ones containing images of the Buddha, and by various decorations such as paper umbrellas in colours. Around this runs the broad pavement or court looking like a street, edged on the outer side by shrines and pagodas, some of them very large, set at all angles, and of very various shapes and designs. Behind these again, to be reached by narrow passages between them, are platforms or rest-houses, looking out over the wide plain below, these are for the use of those who come to worship. On festival days the platforms are crowded with whole families, who bring their bedding, and cooking-pots, and settle down in great enjoyment.

When we stepped on to the great platform or court

* " Burma : a Handbook," by Sir J. G. Scott, K.C.I.E.

the now familiar feeling of bewilderment was strong upon me, there was so much to see, everything was so irregular, so individual, I did not know how to take it all in. This is I suppose a very common feeling with visitors to the Shwe Dagôn; it stuns one by its intricate beauty. We were opposite to the first large shrine and from its dim recesses two shiny brass machine-made faces of images of the Buddha glared at us. A number of priests were kneeling, swaying to and fro, repeating a weird monotonous chant, which seemed a repetition of the same words again and again. White Buddhas with sly sensual faces peered out from the shadows on each side, it was a veritable cave of images, and many little candles guttering in the draught were shining through a low tunnel upon another, the most sacred of all. We should have been obliged to crouch to enter that tunnel, and all we could see without doing so was a glint of the gilt on the immovable image. It is a curious thing that though the images of the Buddha are supposed to be alike, they are most emphatically different. The expression is sometimes sensual, sometimes smirking, sometimes sly, sometimes powerful, and at the best serene and dignified. The newer figures, with the machine-made brass-cast faces, are very uninteresting. By far the most usual position is that of the seated Buddha, when his right hand rests on the right knee with the fingers hanging down, and the left hand is open on his lap. This represents him sitting under the Bo-tree, when there came to him the supreme wisdom. The standing images show him in the attitude of teaching, with the right hand upraised, and the

lying down ones as he was at death when he attained
Nehban, eternal rest, removed from all earthly dis-
turbances.

The platform at the base of the pagoda is so large
that even to walk round it takes a long time, and to
stop continually, as one wishes to, involves still more.
We could not stay longer than about an hour this first
evening, and I only got a general impression, but I
returned subsequently many times to fill in details.
The chief beauty of the Shwe Dagôn is of course the
magnificent centre-piece or tope, which is always
majestic and never tawdry. The strange curves speak
to one, for the language of curves is as that of sounds
and is understood by those who know. The pagoda is
as articulate as music, and when the setting sun shines
on it, making it ruddy gold, as it did that first evening,
there seems to be a deep rich note of hopes fulfilled and
serenity attained, while in the morning light it is sharper
and shriller, telling of the joy of childhood and of the
threshold of life, a radiant joy. The plinth of the
pagoda is of tiers and blocks, its bell-shaped body rises
full and round, then tapers to the spire, and on the top
is a htee or so-called umbrella, not unlike the pope's
tiara, made of metal and gilded. Very few realise the
wealth that devotion has lavished on this beautiful
work, for the part of the pagoda which is wholly covered
with plates of thin solid gold is large, and besides this
the whole is overlaid with gold leaf. The htee is
enriched with bells and with jewels, many of them real ;
and in the sunlight occasionally a ruby or emerald burns
out, scintillating and throbbing in rays of colour. The

IN THE COURTS OF THE SHWE
DAGÔN PAGODA

S. H. Reynolds

SACRED UMBRELLAS, SHWE DAGÒN PAGODA

htee alone cost nearly £50,000 and was a gift of Mindon Min, the last King of Burma but one.

The forest of smaller pagodas rising around the base seems there but to show off the stately majesty of the central one. But these pagodas and the shrines also are so marvellously worked, and so richly decorated, that they are well worth studying. The detail is endless ; looking down the vista of any of the " streets " one sees all the pinnacles and carving and htees in mighty disarray ; wood-work, silver and stone, tinsel and paint, and mirror-work, flash and flicker against a background of stately palms. Every here and there are tall posts highly decorated and terminating in the figure of a bird, the Brahminical duck, with long streamers and pennons of coloured paper flying out from them in the light breeze. These are praying columns, set up to propitiate the nats or spirits.

Some of the shrines are marvellously carved in wood left its natural colour, and others have the wood-work gilded. The most characteristic, and, apparently from the worshippers' point of view, the most effective, are those made of a mosaic of little bits of looking-glass set in zinc. Others are painted a rich terra cotta, the colour of the roads. Some are fantastic in the Chinese style, and some of the pagodas are of plain stone, and moulder away uncared for. Seen as a whole, in the burnished light of an unclouded sun at mid-day, the gilt and tinsel, the tawdriness and overloaded ornament, often shout aloud to the silencing of the grander lines ; but to me they never were so blatant as to drown all noise except their own, for I was fortunate, my first impressions were

E

gained in the dusk of evening, when the stridency is hushed
and only the deeper undertones of grandeur remain.

That first evening I was too much occupied by the
pagoda itself and its attendant shrines to give much
notice to the people.   Besides, darkness was falling and
the colours of their clothes were not noticeable, but
when I came again in the broad light of morning with a
camera, all the gay daintiness of dress of which I had
heard so much shone out radiantly.   I was not alone,
for I was provided with a stalwart chuprassie over six
feet high, who could not speak a word of English, and
who, until I got used to him, embarrassed me a good
deal more than I embarrassed him.   The way in which
he " shoo-ed " the people away from before me as I
walked up the steps, the air with which he held my
camera or sunshade when I was not using them, and the
gesticulations with which he called my attention to any
particularly garish bit of mosaic work, were enough to
destroy the nerve of all but the most self-contained.   He
seemed quite unable to understand I could want to
photograph the ordinary people, and I could not explain.
Presently, however, my difficulties were lightened by a
small, a very small, Burman, who wandered gently up,
and, without being asked, attached himself to my suite
as interpreter.   He explained to the chuprassie it was
chiefly figure-groups I was interested in; he told the
people to stand still for me, but even with his assistance
it was not easy to get good subjects.   There were few
people about and they nearly all knelt or sat in the deep
shadows of the shrines and porticoes.   My friend told me
this lack of worshippers was because there was a festival

on the morrow, when I had better come again, which I
said I would do.   When I did appear the next day I
found him there as gentle and smiling as before.   He
told me his name was Moung Nyun and that he was a
drawing-master.   He proudly brought out a sketch-book
in which he had been making studies of the wood-work
in the pagoda arcade, and he accompanied me so
simply and naturally that I felt he was doing it out
of pure courtesy and not from any idea of tip-hunting
whatever.

But the people, though more numerous on this second
day, were as elusive as ever : in France or England sunshine is enjoyable rather than otherwise, many a group
can one catch unawares for a snap-shot sunning themselves in a street or on the broad steps of an old church,
but in Burma, except in the early morning, when they
love to squat down warming their backs in the sun, the
people prefer the shade, and satisfactory groups are impossible.   I could not interrupt their devotions in the
dark shadows of the shrines to ask them to keep still,
and yet to take them instantaneously was hopeless.   If
ever I did persuade one or other to go into the sun, the
stiffness of the pose completely spoiled any interest in
the photo, so the net result of several mornings' work
was not great.

It is almost hopeless to attempt to give a description
of the people ; there were little boys with their hair cut
all round in a neat fringe, leaving the centre part a
rather skimpy bunch of ends tied tightly and waving
upward like carrot-tops.   The favourite colour beyond
all question is pink, and I cannot describe it otherwise

than as the pinkest of pinks, the kind of colour one sees
as a rule only in cocoa-nut sweets or ice creams.   Blues
and greens were simply non-existent here, though up-
country I came across a few.   No doubt fashion in
colours accounts for something, but it may also be that
the sallow-faced Burman instinctively feels that blues
and greens do not suit his complexion.   The men and
women alike wear lyungis for workaday use, that is to
say, skirts shaped like sacks open at both ends; the
fulness is crossed over and tucked in neatly on one side
by the women, and gathered more in a bunch by the
men.   Their short jackets are also very similar, and
though the men have often moustaches I do not think I
saw a beard on a Burman the whole time I was in Burma;
in fact, the only difference by which one can tell the
sexes is that the man is never seen without his turban,
generally pink, and the woman has her hair uncovered.
He twists his scarf round his head, very often leaving a
sort of bird's nest of dark hair in the middle; she greases
hers, smoothes it up tightly, and carries it in a flat coil
immediately across over the forehead, and there is always
a flower of some sort hanging down on the left side.
An ornamental comb is a favourite addition, or a gold
bangle encircling the coil.   Out of doors and at festivals
the better dressed women complete their costumes by a
light gauzy scarf thrown round the shoulders as English-
women wear them.   The smartest dress of all is a
tamein which occasionally replaces the lyungi: this is
open at one side and shows the leg slightly as the owner
walks, but I saw very few tameins and a great many
lyungis.   The Burmese girl at her smartest smears her

A GROUP OF SHRINES, SHWE DAGÔN PAGODA

ON THE STEPS OF A SHRINE,
SHWE DAGÓN PAGODA

face with a kind of paste called thanaka, which makes it saffron yellow, and wears an immense number of diamonds all over her little person. She swaggers inimitably as she holds out a huge cheroot in her gold-bangled hand. The man's festival garment is a putsoe, a very rich and full silk skirt gathered up in a great bunch. It is said that occasionally the surplus is flung over the shoulder; this I never saw, though I was lucky enough to see the most gorgeous putsoes at the races; one large stout man—stout Burmans are not at all uncommon—had a most radiant pink silk putsoe which must have taken an untold number of yards of silk in the making.

But even at the festival I did not see many smart costumes at the pagoda; there were numbers of poorer folk in check cotton lyungis, above which the brown skin showed at the waist below the jacket, which was sometimes figured with a little sprig like a housemaid's gown. A particularly hideous magenta check seemed the favourite pattern with the men, and often a much worn short coat of European pattern replaced the engie; a weather-stained umbrella was a constant adjunct. All the women walk splendidly, which is no doubt because from earliest childhood they carry chatties and other heavy things on their heads, and in the wide alleys of the Shwe Dagôn their royal walk is seen to great advantage. Their slippers are heelless and very heavy, with a leather sole; the toe-cap is made either by a simple cross band or is of velvet; the difficulty of keeping these shoes on is probably the reason of the sliding step or shuffle so often to be noticed. These shoes are sometimes so absurdly small that the little toe must perforce remain outside the cap, and the heel falls beneath the instep. Stockings are not worn by the women.

There was so much to see at the pagoda that I could have wandered all day about its courts. In one place there was a man with a kind of draught-board before him trying to tempt the people to come and stake on it; he rattled coins together and called out in a loud voice occasionally; what the nature of the gamble was I could not find out. Also there was a clever lean-faced fortune-teller, who dealt out horoscopes on palm-leaf fibre marvellously engraved with weird devices made by a sharp point. His face inspired respect, and I had my fortune told from my hand; the interpreter translated much which was satisfactory, including one characteristic item that I was going to have "plenty money to buy el'phants." There was a man sitting at a stall selling water to drink; there were nuns with shaven heads looking exactly like men, and poongyis or monks in yellow robes. This particular colour, a rather dull but intense yellow, is a relief among so much pink and red.

When I at last tore myself away from the pagoda, I saw yet one other sight on the way home, for I met a dancing, yelling crowd, with bells ringing and flags waving. From the noise and the beating of tom-toms I thought it was some festival procession. In the midst was a canopy of scarlet with little pennons fluttering from it, and at the end of each pennon was a bell which rang in the wind. All of a sudden I had a glimpse of an emaciated, still body, so scantily covered that the sharp outlines were plain to see beneath that canopy, and at one end, uncovered and raised, the sunken face of a corpse of a ghastly hue—the native brown turned sickly green.   A more gruesome contrast could hardly have been found than this affectation of merriment and that poor clay.   It was a Hindu funeral.

CHAPTER III

BURMESE LADIES AT HOME

Across the grey waters of the Gulf of Martaban, nearly
a day's journey by steamer, lies Moulmein, once the
headquarters of the English occupation, when, after the
first Burmese War, England held only Arakan and
Tenasserim. It was seven o'clock in the morning when
we started from the wharf after a rather cheerless
awakening before the sun was up. Even under the
blue sky and strong sun of midday the waters of the
gulf are never anything but grey, owing to the mud and
silt brought down by the waters of the three great rivers,
the Irrawaddy, Sittang, and Salween. It was four in the
afternoon before we came in sight of the high green
ridge upon the slopes of which Moulmein is built,
and the scene grew more and more interesting as we
approached. In midstream were one or two steamers
on which coolies were loading teak ; their brown bodies
and red loin-cloths and turbans glowed bright in the
sunlight. The water front was edged with unlovely
mills and wharves, including a large one belonging to
the Bombay Burma Trading Corporation, of which my
host was a manager. Behind these the houses were
dotted about amid a fine growth of trees right up the

THE GAMESTER

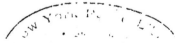

MAH KIN LE AND DAUGHTER (*p.* 52)

slopes of the ridge, which ran parallel with the river,
and was crowned with no less than three groups of
pagodas.   I could see at once that Moulmein might be
a much pleasanter place to live in than Rangoon, and I
hoped I should see as much as I wanted to of the
inside of Burman life.   I had an advantage in this, an
advantage that many people who have lived for years
in the country cannot command, for my hostess, Mrs.
M., had made friends with the best class of Burmese
ladies, and regularly called upon them, and invited
them to see her, a thing that very few Europeans would
think of doing.   It is, indeed, owing to her help in this
and in many other things that I was able to get an idea
of the life of the people at all.

It is really surprising, considering the intrinsic
interest of Moulmein, and the many excursions that
may be easily made from it, how few people find their
way there.   What tourists come to the country at all
almost invariably stay a day in Rangoon, go on up to
Mandalay and back by the river ; ten or twelve days is
considered enough for Burma, and yet if they only took
the trouble to find out how much they miss by this
rush, they would probably stay longer.   The steamers
across the gulf are very comfortable, and run three times
a week.   In the town is a boarding house, " Salween
House," and a dâk bungalow, and though the accommodation is not brilliant it will serve.

At the wharf was a babbling crowd through which
we had to pass before we drove away to Mrs. M.'s
bungalow. This stood high above Salween Park, which
is very like an English park in general, though the trees

F

are all of different kinds from ours. Later I learned
to recognise some of them : banyan, gold mohur, amherstia, padouk, and so on. The bungalow itself is very
pretty, built, as they almost all are, of rich dark brown
teak-wood, which has a grain in it like oak. In front
stood two glorious masses of contrasting colour, a large
bush of plumbago simply covered with blossom, and a
huge poinsettia much higher than a tall man. The
whole of the front of the bungalow is open, and a staircase leads from the lower verandah to the upper one,
which is used as the sitting-room. In the rains heavy
mat blinds fill in the open sides, but while I was there,
except for the roof overhead we might have been out of
doors. The bedrooms all open into one another, and
each has its bath-room or bath-closet attached. The
Anglo-Burman bathroom is very simple, but not at all
inconvenient. There is generally a large oval tin bath
—though sometimes one only gets a wooden tub—two
or three great earthenware chatties full of cold water,
to be ladled out by a dipper as required, and the sweeper
brings up the hot water by an outside staircase when he
has heated it in kerosene tins over a wood fire in the
compound. The floor is of wood or cement, there is
nothing to spoil, and you may splash as you like. In
fact in some bathrooms, built out on piles from the side
of the bungalow, holes are bored in the floor to let the
surplus water run away like a shower bath beneath !
And in one place at least where the bathroom was on
the ground, the same end was achieved by simply
emptying the bath on to the floor and letting it sink in
or stream off as it pleased ! Kerosene tins are a staple of

life in Burma, they are used in almost every conceivable
capacity.   The native carries water in them ; he uses
them as cauldrons in which to heat it ; he ladles out
water with them ; he keeps stores in them ; he even
occasionally packs his small belongings in one when he
travels, using it as a portable trunk ! Up at Bhamo I
saw a house built of kerosene tins flattened out.   It is
an awful thing to think what would happen if the imported oil were suddenly to be sent into the country in
bottles or in some other form of receptacle.   That no
taps are found in the ordinary bungalow goes without
saying, every drop of water has to be carried up from
the well in the compound if there is one, and if that
runs dry, then from the nearest hydrant ; but it is a
country where labour is cheap : it is one man's life-work
to carry water, and nothing is thought about it.   For
drinking purposes every house has a filter, but soda
water is almost universally used, and is half the price it
is in England.

While I stayed at Moulmein we had the French
hours for meals, which I found so convenient that
afterwards when I travelled about alone I adopted
them.   That is to say, they are convenient in a country
where the middle of the day is too hot to work in
comfort, they would not do at all in England.   We
had chota hazri, with some addition such as potted
meat or an egg, before rising ; *dejeuner* at 11.30 or 12 ;
tea about 4.30, and dinner at 8.   This gives one the
opportunity of using all the available time in the day.
The servants, who are natives of India, are hired on a
totally different system from ours.   They get their own

food; in some places an allowance of rice is made to them, but they do not use the house food at all. They sleep out in a go-down in the compound. They have no days off. The "butler" is the most important, and receives from twenty-five to thirty rupees a month; under him there may be a second "boy," who gets about twenty rupees; but in many houses there are just the butler and the "chokrah," who acts as second boy, helps to wait at table and goes messages. The native cook gets about twenty-five rupees per month, the ayah about twenty. The ayah in this family was a most hardworking little woman; she rather embarrassed me by laying hands on every available garment and washing it and hanging it on the back verandah to dry in the sun. At first I was often at a loss, and turned everything upside down in a hasty search for the missing thing, but at last I learnt to be quite sure I should find it hanging on the rail near the big mango in which the crows sat and squawked like parrots. Some of these ayahs are wonderful masseuses, the art being passed from mother to daughter; this one was no exception to the rule. I had had a blow on my heel from a skittle-ball on board ship, and it still hurt me. I showed it to her, but instead of massaging the actual spot, she ran her fingers up to a most painful muscle or ligament, of which I had not before been aware, and kneaded it so determinedly that it was not exactly enjoyable. Still, in three days she did it a vast amount of good. She seemed to have the same intuitive knowledge of bones, joints, and muscles as the "bone-setters," and I was told that she was not exceptional. She was always full of mystery, coming and going like a shadow, stealing into my room with her finger on her lip. She could not speak a word of English. One day she came and knelt in a little heap outside my mosquito curtains and poured out a low mumble of Burmese which, of course, I could not understand, but at last I caught the word "kelow," which I knew meant baby; in fact, it was and is the only Burmese word I know, and I guessed she wanted to show me her baby, of which I had heard. So I signified assent and she hastened away to return presently with as poor a little shrivelled mite as ever I saw. It looked almost too wizened and monkey-like to be human. Its father was some wretched lad who had gone off leaving wife and child. It was difficult not to show in my face the repulsion with which the poor little thing inspired me, while the mother looked down on it in the tenderest pride. The little woman never could understand that I spoke no Burmese ; she always seemed to think, if she only talked enough, some of it would penetrate, and she emphasised all she said by quick nods and abundant gestures. She was a good, energetic little soul.

The three lowest indoor servants are the sweeper, who does the dirty work, the panni-wallah, who brings the water for baths, and the cook's matey, who helps where he is told. Of these the sweeper is always of the lowest caste. Their wages vary from about seven to fourteen rupees a month.

The outdoor servants include coachman and syce : also the dhobi, or washing man, who in all better families is regularly engaged at about twenty-five rupees a month, in addition to his soap; he does the washing in the compound, and gets up muslins and frills amazingly well considering his limited resources. It is just as well to have your clothes done under your own inspection, for some of the washing-places where the village dhobies do congregate, to clash the garments on the stones, the universal substitute for a "posh-tub," are anything but clean, and a horrible ailment called dhobi-itch is common. Many of the dhobies I saw were attractive-looking men clad in spotless linen. At Moulmein I could look out of my window and see the house dhobi, all in white with silver bangles on his wrists, beating the clothes on two stones, while beside him was the panni-wallah clothed in a red loin-cloth, with gold earrings and a chignon, drawing water from the well, and near at hand was a picturesque group of plantains.

The price of washing to an outsider is reasonable enough, about five rupees a hundred pieces, but it should be arranged beforehand, as the men will ask any price they think they can get. One can generally have washing done in a day or two if moving on, but it is always well to employ a dhobi recommended by some one.

The dhursi, or tailor, is not an invariable adjunct to a house; but a lady very often has her own dhursi, and pays him from twenty-five to thirty rupees a month. The dhursies seemed to me, as a rule, not nearly so attractive as the dhobies; they were often coarse and greasy-looking. They are very quick-fingered, and copy anything set them marvellously, but are quite unable to originate or suggest. The malli, or gardener, has not the same standing as his kind in England; he probably acts for several houses, and part of his work is to cut grass for the horses by contract. Then there is the derwan, or night watchman, an important functionary in a country where there are no front doors to lock and the verandah is the living-room, open to any one. It is doubtful if the derwan has ever done much, but the knowledge that he is there, and *may* be awake, probably acts preventively in a land where men are not very brave.

What I enjoyed most of all during my delightful time at Moulmein was meeting Burmese ladies on social terms. On Christmas Day, as we were coming back from an early service in church—where punkahs were kept swinging, where nearly every one wore topees, and the decorations were almost wholly of pink and white roses—we encountered the principal Burmese lady in Moulmein, Mah Shwe Bwin, and her adopted son and daughter-in-law coming up to call. Mah Shwe Bwin means Mrs. Golden Blooming. In Burmese courtesy-titles a woman is always Mah, which means either Mrs. or Miss; an old woman is, however, called Amaigyi. A young Burman is at first a lugale, or boy; then he is addressed as Moung, which really means brother, but has come to signify Mr.; after about forty years of age a man is addressed as Ko, and still older as Oo; if he grow to be very old and very much respected he is Apogyi; whereas any one who builds a rest-house has the title of Zeyat Payah—Zeyat meaning a rest-house —and any one who builds a shrine, is Payah Tagah. Burmese words have so many different meanings that it

is often difficult to fix the exact intention of a name;
for instance, the little house ayah was Mah Mo, which
might mean either Mrs. or Miss, Mushroom, Rain, or
Roof! Mah Shwe Bwin I quickly learned to love and
respect; she is one of the real old aristocrats of Burma,
and in her manners and appearance you feel all the time
that she is a gentlewoman. I never met any one else
with whom to compare her while I was in the country.
She is a widow and enormously rich, owning mills and
transacting business matters; but she cannot speak
English, and has always to have an interpreter.
Luckily in Moulmein this is not difficult, for so many
of the young Burmans attend the English schools that
nearly all boys of fifteen or so speak English. Mah
Shwe Bwin was very plainly dressed, without a scrap of
jewellery, for it is the custom for the Burmese ladies to
pass their jewellery on to their daughters-in-law when
they arrive at about forty, which is comparatively much
older than with us, as married life begins about sixteen.
She was dressed in a dark bronze flowered lyungi, and a
little white jacket, with a pretty scarf of light muslin,
covered with green spots, thrown over her shoulders,
and she wore pink satin shoes with a divided strap
passing between the first two toes. The adopted son
was a short fat man, in a gorgeous pink silk putsoe of
a large check pattern. He had left his patent-leather
shoes and silk socks at the foot of the staircase. The
wearing of European shoes by " Young Burma " makes
this matter of shoe-dropping a difficult one; but, in
spite of this, no really well-mannered Burman would
think of coming into a room, where there were ladies,

MAH SHWE BWIN

MAH SHWE BWIN AT THE DOOR
OF HER SHRINE (*p.* 56)

in shoes, any more than a well-mannered Englishman
would come in wearing a hat. Here, as in so many
other cases, the newer code is ousting the older one and
giving nothing in place of it. A Burman cannot
remove his turban, in fact this in itself would be an act
of disrespect ; yet he keeps on his English shoes, and so
discards his own manners without replacing them by
ours. It is also not considered polite for a man to sit in
the presence of ladies, and I must say Mah Shwe Bwin's
son was very polite. However, he was not agile in the
English tongue, and as an interpreter lacked a good
deal; to me, unaccustomed to Burmese methods, to
have to carry on the conversation in scraps with a man
who stood all the time was constraining. Indeed, I
found this matter of conversation a great difficulty.
Topics were strictly limited, the replies were even more
so, and it was impossible to go on asking questions all
the time. The old lady had brought plantains, oranges,
fancy biscuits, and a cake in a tin box as presents, and
when we had discussed these and a few other things I
stopped altogether, and yet there was so much I wanted
to ask our guests. If I could have talked direct to the old
lady herself how much better I could have got on ! At
last, as a happy thought, I brought in some Burmese silks
I had bought, and this aroused interest; they examined
them all carefully, fingering them, trying the texture and
asking the price, which is always a polite thing to do.
I was pleased to hear I had paid "not too much." The
silk I had got to make up into a lyungi for myself
attracted special attention ; it was of a glorious red-gold
or nasturtium colour, which would have been quite

impossible to match in England. I asked how I should judge what width of material to use for the lyungi, and was told the correct thing was to take as much as would go folded round the waist, and as much again as reached, doubled, to the tip of the middle finger, when the elbow was pressed in to the waist, in fact the old measure of a cubit. At length, as I had hoped, the ladies kindly offered to take away the silk and make the garment for me, for which I was very grateful, as then I was sure it would be correctly done. I then asked if I might take a photo of Mah Shwe Bwin, and after some gentle protest, on the ground that her clothes were not good enough, she consented, and we went into the sunlight of the lower verandah.

Unfortunately the photograph, though clear, does not give any idea of that wise, shrewd, kindly face. When we shook hands, English fashion, in parting, she asked us to come and see her, and promised to take us to see the shrine which she was having built.

She subsequently carried out her promise of making me the lyungi, and sent it to me, and then, finding she had inadvertently retained a piece of the silk which was over, she returned it with the following little note, evidently written for her by her son or grandson :

"DEAR MADAM,—I am very sorry to forget to send this pease of cloth. Now I saw in my box at once I send to you. Please excuse me. I close my letter with loved.

"MAH SHWE BWIN."

Anything more gloomy and uncomfortable than a

wealthy Burman's house it would be hard to find; they seem to have adopted all the worst features of the English house and discovered none of its comfort. I went with Mrs. M. one day to call on some very wealthy Burmans, money-lenders, who were not aristocrats like Mah Shwe Bwin, but had made their money recently. The house outside looked like a square solid brick-and-cement mansion in an early Victorian style in two stories. There was a sort of verandah or stoep in front roofed in, and from this the front door opened immediately into the living-room, which occupied the whole area between the principal four walls. There was no window in it at all, and the only light came from the front door. On the far side of the room was a corresponding door leading to back premises, and very dark. The room was paved with cement, and was very high and dismal. There was a round wooden table, that might in England be used for a kitchen table, in the middle, and several hard-backed chairs and a few small sofas, covered with dust-cloths, set back against the wall, as a concession to European taste. The Burman, of course, always prefers to sit on the floor; it is only the boys at the English schools who are learning the use of seats. One corner of the room was partitioned off, and we were told that there lay the master of the house, who was ill. The Burman has a very strong prejudice against having any one's feet over his head, and consequently the upper storey is not used when it is avoidable; yet here a wooden staircase or ladder led upward through a sort of trap in the ceiling, so perhaps some members of the family slept upstairs.

We had not forewarned our friends of our coming,
and consequently caught them unawares, but even then
the daughter, who is about eighteen and newly married,
was wearing double diamonds as a species of links all
down the front of her little engie, and each one was as
large as a finger-nail. I could not believe at first they
were diamonds, but was assured of it, as no Burman
would wear any imitation jewellery. They were probably not of the first water, might be yellowish in colour,
but diamonds they were. Otherwise she was not prettily
dressed, and she promised to come and see us when she
had all her jewellery and best clothes on, a promise she
kept. She seemed a mere little doll, fit only for the
wearing of jewellery, and was a contrast to her sensible-
looking mother.

My visit to Burma dissipated finally the idea of the
Burman girls being " pretty " according to our ideas.
They are sometimes dear coquettish little things, with a
great deal of charm and some personality, but to apply
the word "pretty" to their broad noses, flat little faces,
thanaka-stained, and to the straight, strained, greased
hair, is a misuse of adjectives. Taking, charming, gracious, alluring, are all in the right place applied to them ;
but not pretty. Sir J. G. Scott expresses this very
well in saying of Japanese and Burmese women alike :
" Both have the power of beauty without the possession
of it."

I found conversation here a difficulty also. There was
a boy of about fifteen, a son of Mah Kin Le, the old lady,
and he interpreted ; but I could not get on easily. The
ladies solemnly inquired my age, where I came from,

TWO BETTER-CLASS BURMESE GIRLS (*p.* 67)

MAIN STREET, MOULMEIN

how much my clothes cost, and several other personal details, and then the silence became oppressive. I in my turn inquired of the boy, whose name was Moung Ba, when he would be married. He told me at about twenty, and that his father would choose his wife, and that afterwards he would go and live at the house of his father-in-law. That he did not learn to do anything particular, because his work in life would be the same as his father's-in-law, and he did not know yet what it would be! That he would be free to say no if he did not like the girl, but he would never in any case see her unchaperoned until they were married. In reply to my questions as to the usual household arrangements, and how the ladies employed themselves, he said they had two meals a day, one at nine in the morning, after which the ladies " prayed " for about an hour, and another at four in the afternoon. That the ladies preserved ginger and sewed to fill up their days. I give his replies un-adorned. It is difficult to gather any but the crudest notions from an Eastern boy speaking in an imperfectly known tongue. Of course one hears always that the married women in Burma do a great deal of business, and even the unmarried girls keep stores in the bazaar ; but Moung Ba told me that after the ear-boring cere-mony, i.e., when she is of a marriageable age, no girl is allowed to go about alone.

We did not stay long here, passing on to fulfil our promise to Mah Shwe Bwin. Her front room was the facsimile of that we had just left, except that very high up on the walls were some marvellous native pictures, done in the most gorgeous colours, and utterly innocent of perspective. They were partly painted, partly worked in silk, and they were lavishly decorated with spangles of gold. Two of these were old and came from Mandalay, she told us. She sat on her chair in a funny little hump with her feet tucked up under her. It is perfectly amazing how the Burmese ladies stow away their lower limbs—they seem reduced to a trunk only, almost as if they had the power of telescoping!

A very pleasant unaffected lad of sixteen undertook the office of interpreter; he told me he was called Moung Api, and I think he was a grandson of Mah Shwe Bwin. He was very simply dressed in a thin merino English vest and cotton lyungi, with his hair cropped like that of an English boy.

The conversation went on something in this style:

" Has Mah Shwe Bwin any daughters ? "

" Yes, three."

" Do they live here ? "

" No—not two."

" In Moulmein ? "

" No."

" Are they married ? "

" They are dead."

Thus abruptly ended that topic. I was told afterwards that "dead" may equally mean disgraced, or dead to family.

In the pause that ensued the old lady said something to the boy, who hesitated and looked at me shyly, but after encouragement he came across and said to me in his soft voice:

" She wants to know what does your husband ? "

"Tell her I have no husband."

On receipt of this information there followed a long silence. The old lady's face became perceptibly more solemn; then she said something, and the boy in his graceful, timid way informed me:

"She says she is praying for you!"

Luckily refreshments appeared at this moment, when it was difficult to preserve a becoming gravity, and formed a welcome break; they consisted of plantains, oranges, lemonade, and for adornment bunches of a small and rather dull orchid, which must have been common, as every little school-child had a spray of it in her hair. Then we were told we might go to see the wonderful shrine Mah Shwe Bwin is building. She and another woman, who seemed a kind of family retainer, or poor relation, and the boy went in a gharry; we followed in the carriage.

We had to dismount at the foot of the ridge and walk up a steep and rugged track, which the frail-looking little old lady took slowly; my heart warmed to her, she looked so small in her tightly-wound lyungi, and her face was so humorous and sensible that I would very willingly have kissed her, and all feeling as between myself and a coloured race had vanished. The ascent was not long, and we came out on to a flat space, where numbers of native coolies, working at the roof of the shrine, were passing up and down a wide bamboo ladder.

So we went in, and saw the great image of a colossal Buddha of shining brass with a gold head. Moung Api explained in awestruck whispers that this was no mask,

but a head of solid gold right through, and for sanctity
none could compare with it but the Buddha in the
Arakan pagoda, near Mandalay. He told me at first
there were 100 viss of gold in the head, but came
back later to correct himself and say he had meant
1000.   One thousand viss equals 365 lb. weight of gold,
and reckoning it at £3 17s. 6d. the ounce this comes
out between £16,000 and £17,000, which is surely
stupendous.   I am told, however, that Mah Shwe Bwin
did not pay for it all herself, though the greater part
came from her ; at the casting, when Mrs. M. was
present, there was a great ceremony, and tremendous
excitement and religious fervour, so that men gave
money and girls tore off their bangles and earrings and
threw them into the melting-pot.

Many offerings of the usual sort were heaped before
the Buddha, who had rather an expressionless face as
Buddhas go, and when I asked the boy what was the
significance of the two hideous figures which stood on
each side, he replied :

"No meaning, only for agreeable."

The light was fast going, but I got a photograph of
the little old lady as she sat crouched up by the door of
her shrine, with a wonderful spiritual fervour in her
expression.   To look at her in her spartan simplicity of
dress, one might have thought her almost a beggar, and
then one remembered the gold so lavishly poured out,
and the contrast was piquant.

As we passed down she suggested we should rest in
one of the rest-houses near, and I asked that I might
go on to the nearest and largest of the three pagodas

THE BOY AND THE BELL, OLD PAGODA
MOULMEIN (*p.* 65)

SCENES IN THE LIFE OF THE BUDDHA
OLD PAGODA, MOULMEIN (p. 65)

on the ridge with Moung Api for guide, while the others waited instead of climbing the terrific flights of stairs that led up to it. I was glad to get this opportunity of talking to an intelligent lad, but I fear I did not make so much of it as another might have done. He told me long tales of nats and beloos (spirits and devils) which I could not follow. He showed me two representations of the latter, real bogies, on the stairway, and said they were the kind that haunted dark woods. He pointed out the tall praying columns, and said they were to the " heaven-born nats." He told me he was very soon going through the novitiate in the priesthood, which every Burman undergoes, and before which he is not considered a man, but an animal. He said some boys went for three months, and seven days was the very least time you could give with self-respect; the probation is generally done during the holidays. I asked him if, when a boy became a real monk, it was because his father willed it, or because he wanted to be one himself, and he replied that, as a rule, it was the father's doing, but the father would not choose a boy who was " not good." He was careful to explain that the Burmans do not worship Buddha, the images are only to remind them and make them think; they do not believe them to be alive. I was rather amused when he launched out on a topic of his own, and said one thing had always puzzled him, and that was that the Englishmen in the I.C.S. who had passed high examinations in Burmese often could not speak it at all. He instanced one man, a friend of my own, in whose office he had been and said, " He has passed very good examina-

H

tions, but he does not speak; not at all; even in the
court he has an interpreter; I do not think he knows."
I did not give the boy away when I met his superior
again! I liked him particularly; he was quite untainted
with the modern affectations, and during all my wanderings, in which I met many Burmese boys, I never
came across one who appealed to me so much as
Moung Api.

Mah Kin Le and her son and daughter were not long
in paying us the promised return call, and when I saw
the girl's jewellery, I was positively startled by it. The
huge diamond links still figured prominently in her
jacket, and she wore also earrings and rings set with
immense stones. Her bangles were flat bars of gold,
a mass of diamonds, and a large diamond pin impaled
her topknot of hair; all these stones are set in a way
that appears to us clumsy, and which certainly does not
show them off to advantage; that is to say, they have
the point outwards, and stand on a sort of little platform of very solid gold, so the effect is that of a miniature pyramid. The daughter, whose name is Mah Mya
Hnit, was, besides her jewellery, excessively smart,
wearing a pink silk-figured lyungi, pink scarf and China
silk engie, diversified by a little blue pattern. Her face
was thickly daubed with thanaka paste, so as to make
her look quite fair; when put on carefully, this stuff is
not offensive, as it has a slightly fragrant smell, but
when left in a clumsy line across the forehead at the
roots of the hair, as is done by many girls, it is like an
ugly mask. Her hair was very shiny and bound into
the tightest little knob. The boy, who had an intelli-

gent face, round bright brown eyes, and rather thick lips, like his sister, was a finished specimen of " Young Burma." He was dressed in a rainbow silk lyungi— for boys do not wear a putsoe until they are married —an ordinary white English shirt, with diamond studs and gold sleeve-links ; over this was a white Burmese jacket. His gold watch chain was very much in evidence, and also his yellow leather lace-up shoes, which he did not remove downstairs. He sat while he talked, and his manners contrasted very unfavourably with those of Moung Api. The older lady smoked a big green cheroot solemnly the whole time she stayed. I offered her and her daughter my own cigarettes and they took them, but the girl did not get on with hers, and after a while Mah Kin Le explained that her daughter was not much of a smoker, and she took the cigarette from her and finished it after her own, resuming later her own green cheroot, which had lain slowly burning on the edge of the table near her all the time ! These cheroots are not made of pure tobacco, but of the pith of a tree which looks like sawdust ; this is mixed with a little tobacco and ginger and perhaps opium, and the peculiar smoke made in burning is sharp and acrid. It is the funniest sight to see the little Burmese ladies making their by no means large mouths into round holes for the insertion of the mighty end. We gave our guests soda water among other refreshments, and when I saw them drink it, I feared they must have thought me sadly lacking in manners, for I did not make the appreciative grumbles and grunts in the truly courteous way after drinking. When I asked them they willingly consented to be photographed, and our going downstairs to take them broke up a sitting which had become almost insupportably wearying, as they stayed nearly two hours. When Mr. M. came in he said that it was our own fault; they could not go until we made the move!

CHAPTER IV

WANDERINGS IN MOULMEIN

THE Oriental cannot understand how any man, much less any woman, can desire to walk about for pleasure; to him the fact of a lady's sauntering about unattended is derogatory to her dignity and implies that she is not of much consequence. I felt this all over Burma in greater or less degree, and chafed under it; up-country I always took the boy with me, and grew sufficiently accustomed to his presence not to mind it, but certainly to walk attended even by a solemn Madrassee has not quite the same charm as being quite alone. In Moulmein and Maymyo I was more free than in other places; Maymyo is so thoroughly English that English customs are accepted unquestioningly, and Moulmein has been so long in the possession of the English, and there are so many Europeans living in it, that English manners and customs are at all events understood. It was therefore not impossible to go about alone, though unusual. The bungalow I was staying in was on the outskirts of the town, which made the matter easier, for the ridge rose straight up behind, so it was attained without having to pass through any streets, and it was a capital place for a walk.

In the early mornings I used to go up there, and look down the other side upon a rolling plain traversed by the river Ataran. Far out in the plain rose huge lumps of detached limestone rock sharp as razors along the top, giving a most peculiar effect; they rose as rocks rise from the sea, sheer without intermediate slopes. In one of these is the famous Farm Caves which I afterwards visited, and many of them are honeycombed with similar caves as yet unexplored.

I used to take the camera with me on these wanderings in case I met any likely subject, but the place was very quiet and I did not often meet any one. Once I saw a bullock cart of the lighter sort driven by a Burman who had his two children with him. I had already grown to recognise a certain type of Burman, the man with a shrewd kindly expression that made you feel you could trust him and make friends with him. This man looked so amiable that I signalled to him to stop, and by gesticulations explained I wanted to take his photo. We carried on the conversation by signs for some minutes, and any one who had seen us thus animatedly conversing in dumb show would have been amused to hear him remark in perfectly good English as the shutter snapped, "Will you send me one?"

The photo came out well and I did send him one; I hope he appreciated it.

One day I wandered down the far side of the ridge into the plain below, I passed two unfinished pagodas guarded by the usual red-eyed leogryphs. By the side of one of them was a large weather-stained gamp umbrella, and the voice of the Burman to whom it belonged came to me in a monotonous sing-song as he made his devotions. The Burman is not supposed to pray Moung Api had told me, but merely to refresh his memory by repeating the law, and he should offer praise, but there is no doubt that their devotions are indistinguishable from prayers. Human nature could not live by repetition and praise alone. Further on I passed a poongyi with his begging bowl on his morning round. At the same time a snake startled me by gliding across the path right under my feet, but a native woman ran to look at it, and showed by signs it was harmless. The plain at the base of the hill was grassy and open, cut up by wheel-tracks and lined by a tangle of scrubby bushes, so that on the whole it had a good deal the appearance of a Surrey common. On examination, however, every single plant and tree is different from those to which we are accustomed, it is only at a distance or in the mass such a delusion is possible. The ground at my feet was covered with large richly coloured deep red pods belonging to a mighty fig-tree. This shaded a group of Zeyats, or rest-houses, put up for the accommodation of those who came to carry out the last ceremonies in connection with their friends' burial, for the Burmese burial-ground was close at hand. The graves were mostly unmarked, but some had hideous heavy altar tombs singularly resembling those to be seen in English churchyards.

I did not however often wander down the hill into the plain, I preferred to walk along the heights of the ridge with the rolling plain lying spread out at my feet

like a map. These heights are crowned by three sets
of pagodas. The nearest of them rises high above the
pathway, and can only be reached by a flight of steep
and precipitous steps of red brick much broken and
worn. The platform surrounding the pagoda is also
old and crumbled, with grass springing up between the
stones. The fascination of the place is indescribable.
I went there many times, for there I could be utterly
alone, perched high on the very crown of the hill, with
the majestic blue distances spreading before me to
seeming infinity. As I sat here on New Year's Day I
could hear the tinkling of the pagoda bells high overhead in the ethereal blue, ringing sharply sweet above
the tearing sound made by the wind in the broad-leaved
palms. Pagoda bells were one of the most satisfactory
fulfilments of anticipation. They are set on the metal
htee or umbrella which crowns the spire of every pagoda
and are rung by the action of the wind as it wafts past
them. The sound is sometimes unheard, for it may be
lost in the noise of the throng below ; and if the pagoda
be in a sheltered spot, the tongues are not easily moved
to utterance, but here, out on the high hillside, with no
scrambling of feet or droning of voices to dull their
magic, they spoke straight to the heart of me, telling I
know not what strange secrets of the East. Sometimes
they clashed all together, and then there was heard
the sleepy tinkle of one dropping to silence, gently
sighing away, but before it quite ceased another rang
out thin, sweet and insistent as if it would be heard, and
quite suddenly the sound broke off—the bells had told
enough !

A BURMESE BURIAL PLACE, MOULMEIN

MOUNG KA IN HIS BULLOCK CART

The old pagoda was once gilt all over, but is now sadly worn and dilapidated; the gold leaf has peeled off, leaving great patches. As I sat and looked at it the far-away voices of the little scholars came faintly wafting upward from the poongyi choung down below, and a salmon-pink flower fell silently from its slender stem on a hybiscus drooping over the parapet near.

I wandered round and peeped into the four shrines which flank the pagoda at the four cardinal points. White and dim images of colossal Buddhas peered back at me.

At various places on the platform are large sacred bells slung between two uprights; a mop-headed boy, who had apparently sprung out of the pavement, consented to stand by one pillar as I photographed the bell. After this he followed me round, and whenever he got a chance peered into the camera at about two inches distance, as if he expected to find a picture of himself there! In a sort of shed running along two sides at an angle is a weird and interesting set of carved wooden figures, about a third life-size, representing scenes in the life of the Buddha. I got a photograph of this too by giving the film a longish exposure. The meaning of the figures I do not know; there are three shiny black ones, almost skeletons, that must have a curious story attached to them.

Further along the ridge, at a considerable distance, is the White pagoda, which is of dome or bell shape, and having been recently re-coated with white chunam, it absolutely shines out against the brilliant sky. I saw it several times, once in the evening, when it glowed with the reflection of the orange-yellow light;

I

huge crows, seated in the niches, looked colossal by the
contrast of their sable on the snow, while the brown skins
of the poongyis and the dusky yellows of their robes
were startling against the purity of the background.
The last and most important pagoda on this ridge is that
I had already visited with Moung Api.   It stands very
high and is reached by steep flights of steps ; those on
the side away from the town are extraordinarily precipitous and make one shudder to look down them.

The sunsets at Moulmein I never saw equalled anywhere else, not even in the Red Sea.   We used often
to drive in the evenings along the Strand or river front,
a broad road which is the fashionable Moulmein pro-
menade.   It is not an attractive place, for, being shut in
by the houses and the ridge on the land side, it gets no
breeze.   The way is rendered perilous by the bicycles
ridden by Eurasian boys and girls, on either side of
the road, without the least regard to rules, and by badly
driven ticca gharries crammed with Burmans, while
the dust rises in clouds.   But the sunsets seen across
the wide river redeem all.   The pink of these is not the
same salmon pink we are accustomed to associate with
sunsets in England, but a rose-coloured flush, often
running into pale yellow.   Well have I since understood
why a particular kind of Jap kimono in yellow silk over
a pink lining is called an " evening sky " kimono. Many
Burmese silks seem to have been steeped in sunsets ;
one of a gorgeous apricot colour, to be bought in
Mandalay, turns lemon-yellow in certain lights, and has
warm shadows, a fact not wholly accounted for by dis-
covering that the threads of the warp are of pink set in

a saffron woof. Occasionally the sunsets took the form of expanding bars of light radiating like the spokes of a wheel, clear cut as red-hot iron.

One morning I begged the services of Mrs. M.'s second " boy "—whom I afterwards engaged as my own retainer—to act as interpreter, and sallied forth into the town to try to get a few photographs of street scenes. Any one who has tried in like circumstances will know the difficulties I had to contend with. The drawback of a too powerful sun was paramount. We would enter a long street and find one side, the sunny side, lying white and bare and deserted, and the other, black by reason of the heavy shadow, alive with people. There were little brown girls with babies on their hips, old grandmothers sitting in doorways, children sprawling in the roadway with pariah dogs, all in deep shade. To stop and ask, through the interpreter, that they would keep still while I took a photograph by exposure, had one of two results: either they fled like frightened rabbits, or the more educated, understanding the camera, stood bolt upright like ramrods and all natural- ness in the picture was lost. If only one were invisible it would not be so difficult, but the sight of my standing ready with the camera was enough to make them all uncomfortable and stiff. At length I saw two well- dressed girls get out of a gharry and go into a store, so I followed them and asked them if they would be taken ; one assented cheerfully, the other required some persuasion, but both were as stiff as bolts when the shutter was snapped. I came across another group after much wandering, and by explaining the situation

through the boy at great length, got them to stand
still.   Just as I was about to take the photo, a proud
father thrust a hideous little native boy of about three
years old, dressed in a peaked cap and a serge sailor
suit three sizes too big for him, and with a startling
hiatus of brown skin between tunic and knickers, into
the middle.   I had to make signs that he should be
taken away, and to salve the parent's feelings explained
that I saw so many boys dressed like that in England
it was not interesting to me.   Further on several girls,
who had been to the bazaar, were sitting on the shady
side of the street with their big baskets at their feet.
I tried to get them to move just a little way into the
sun.   They laughed merrily, shaking their heads
violently, and as the refusal was evidently dictated by
coyness, I wasted a good deal of persuasion on them ;
by the time I gave them up in despair and turned away
I found the whole street blocked by a deeply interested
and attentive crowd, mostly composed of native coolies.
I hailed a gharry to get out of it, and let the gharry wallah
go where he pleased.   Some distance away I passed a
better class house and saw some well-to-do people with
two children outside.   I was getting desperate at the
small result of such a tedious morning's work, so I
stopped the gharry, jumped out, and began the usual
explanations. These people were quite willing to
oblige me and responded at once, even understanding
my attempt to pose them by making one child sit
down. The younger one, by a delightful childish
gesture of nervousness at the moment of being taken,
made a very natural picture.   Then we went on once

NATIVE QUARTERS, MOULMEIN

UNFINISHED PAGODA, MOULMEIN (*p.* 63)

more, the boy hanging on at the back of the gharry, and presently came into the native quarter, a part almost wholly given over to the natives of India, with rows of similar tenements, open in front almost like sheds. On one of these I saw advertised in English, " Lodging-house for twenty persons, four rooms." As the whole building was of the smallest, presumably one room was divided into four by extempore partitions. But so much of the life is carried on in the roadway that floor space is not essential. In the mornings the people perform their own or their children's toilets in full view of all the passers-by. Truth to tell, there is not much toilet to make where the children are concerned ; a little check shirt, ending just where, according to European notions, it should begin, was quite a grand dress ; many of the little round-bodied, beady-eyed imps had nothing on at all save a string of beads and few silver bangles. In the evenings groups of them surround the hydrants, with their lank black hair falling in soaked rats'-tails, their bare brown bodies shining with the wet, dancing beneath the welcome gush of cool water. Even men and women come to the hydrants, though they always keep on their garments, which, being of cotton, are none the worse for a wash at the same time as their owners. The little Burman girls of six or seven wear lyungis like their parents, and it is a comical sight to see them drawing them up and tucking them in with all the skill and nonchalance of their mothers.

The delights of Moulmein were many and varied ; one was my first introduction to a box-wallah or native

silk merchant, who brings round his wares to the
bungalows and untying mighty bales on the verandah
converts it into a sea of billowy waves of colour.   The
man who came regularly to Mrs. M.'s house was a
swarthy ruffian called Sirroomull, a clever trader and
one honest according to his lights—or his self-interest.
He turned up one morning attended by two almost
naked coolies, who carried his goods, and when we
went down to the verandah we found him there complacently settled for the whole day if we liked—no
hurry—the joy of sales lies in the bargaining, and the
Oriental would feel sadly defrauded of his rights if the
mem-sahib did not know enough to argue with him;
the pleasure of carrying off the money of a greenhorn
would hardly be compensation for the utter dulness of
the transaction.

I would have been that greenhorn, but I had luckily
the advice of one well skilled in trading and prices, and
it was as good as a play to hear the desultory conversation that went on between my friend and Sirroomull,
each side feigning perfect indifference as to the result.

It ran something in this way :

" How much that green Bokhara silk ? "

" That, mem-sahib, very good silk, most rich, it three
rupees a yard," he unrolled a length of glorious coloured
material.

" Three rupees?   I never heard of such a thing !
Why I get as good as that in Rangoon for two ; besides
it is not a good colour, and there is a mark on it."

" Men-sahib has said," the man laid it aside as if the
matter were ended, and rolled out with a flourish of

his hand a soft cloud of blue chiffon-like material.
" That pineapple silk, mem-sahib."

" Yes, I know ; it does to trim hats, but it's very
flimsy. How much ? "

" That, mem-sahib, is one rupee the yard."

" A rupee ! I'll give you eight annas."

" Well, mem-sahib, just for luck, to begin buy, mem-
sahib shall have for eight annas the yard, how many ? "
He measured the piece. " There are seven yards and
a half."

" I don't want more than seven ; you can give me
in the extra bit if you like."

He looked unutterable reproach, but tossed the piece
aside as bought, and so it went on with long intervals
during which neither side said anything at all. We
departed to have breakfast, and returned to find the
man still there and immovable, and the waves of
colour still illuminating the shadows of the verandah.
There was glorious silver-blue Burmese silk, enough
for a dress, for eighteen rupees ; it lay against the dull
green Bokhara ; there was a rich Canton tussore gleaming against a peculiarly royal flame colour ; saffron was
intermingled with pale mauve ; it seemed as if the man
knew how to make each colour yield its best by placing
it near its complement, though his hand apparently
threw so carelessly. He had not only Burmese silks,·
but others from Japan, India, China, and much glorious
handworked stuff, such as a kimono covered with
butterflies every one different in design ; and a pure
silk blouse-length with daintily worked storks in flight
across the front.

The peculiarity of the Burmese silks is, say those who have tested them, that they never "cut," and that the colours stay fast through any amount of washing; this no doubt is because they are handmade, and the dyes are pure vegetable. English-bought silks in Burma are hopeless, they go directly to tatters and rags.

In the end I spent a great deal more than I had intended to do, but as, on an average, we got each article at about two-thirds the price the man asked, and generally had the best part of a yard thrown in, I do not think we did badly. But I did not get all my silks from Sirroomull; for some I went to the bazaar.

The bazaar is a wonderful sight; it is dirty, noisy, crowded, but it was one of the places where I learned the most, and seemed to get right down among the people as I did nowhere else.

The front, which is in the principal street, looks like a row of untidy stalls or open shops; there are sacks, and bottles, and barrels, and every sort of litter blocking the spaces between these, which give access to the bazaar. Inside, the building is a mighty raftered shed, very dark, but airy. The ground is dirty and uneven, so that we had to take some care where we stepped, and our movements were hampered by a rapidly growing crowd of coolies, each with a huge basket, competing for the job of carrying any goods we might buy. In the interests of peace and quiet, as well as to prevent our heels being too closely followed, we selected one young stripling, slim and well-formed, wearing all his worldly wealth in the form of a belt of silver discs.

The bazaar is divided into alleys lined by a kind of

OUR COOLIE OUTSIDE THE BAZAAR
MOULMEIN

BURMESE GIRL IN BAZAAR, MOULMEIN

continuous raised divan, on which the traders sit cross-
legged with their wares on shelves behind them.   This
was so, at least, in the first section, where cloths, and
silks, and prints, and other materials were sold.   A
great many of the men keeping these stalls were natives
of India, and among them the most popular costume
appeared to be an English white shirt worn outside a
lyungi or a pair of trousers.   Though we experienced a
good deal of jostling and crowding in the bazaar, none
of it was rude or intentional; it was either because the
people were so anxious to get a look at us, or because
they were pressed on by others from behind, and they
were all most good-humoured and smiling.   We were
the only Europeans present, and I should judge that
the place was seldom visited by Europeans.   It differs
altogether from the large, clean, well-lighted building
at Mandalay, where any European can walk with perfect ease.

At Moulmein I was fortunate enough to have with
me a lady who was as much at home in Hindustanee as
in English, who knew every turn and stall in the bazaar,
and who was the personification of good-temper.   She
helped me to choose the silk I wanted for a lyungi and
told me the value of the material, which was a thick
rough quality, generally sold in lengths of three yards
for this purpose.   The two lengths I eventually bought
were both shot with gold in a wonderful way, though
the ground of one was nasturtium colour and the other
a deep lilac; for these I paid six rupees each.   While
the bargaining over the transaction went on the owner
of the stall sat in apparent indifference, merely indicating

by the faintest perceptible nod whether he agreed to any price when his assistant turned to him for directions.

Then we passed on into the grain department, where the stalls were nearly all kept by Burmans, many of them girls, and at our appearance the excitement was great. It rose to fever-pitch, and there was a regular buzz, when I borrowed a high stool, for I had no tripod, and, propping up the camera, made ready to take a photo of a little Burmese girl sitting on piled-up sacks in charge of great bowls of grain. She was smoking an enormous cheroot, but put it down and looked on most composedly at my preparations, evidently enjoying her importance immensely. I signed to her to take the cheroot up again, and requested her to keep still as I had to give the photo a long exposure. When I had finished I turned to behold one of the most amazing sights : not only were the alley-ways thronged with an eager crowd, but on all points of vantage, steps, shelves, stalls, even rafters, up to the very roof, was a semicircle of dark half-clad figures, punctuated by white teeth and gleaming eyes. If I could only have taken the scene as I saw it then ! But even as I looked they melted away magically.

We passed on, seeing displayed for sale all sorts of queer things : bowls full of tiny seeds called *tele*, to be ground into oil ; the bark of the tree from which thanaka, the favourite face-paste, is made, ground up and mixed with water. It is said to be very cooling in cases of prickly heat, but that is not why the girls wear it ; it is because they wish to appear fair. A grinning old poongyi, with hollows like pits appearing on his skinny

shoulders, begged from us; I must say this was an
isolated instance; poongyis are not supposed to have any
money, and I was never asked for alms even when I
penetrated into their monasteries.

From the drug store, smelling with the condensed
odour of seventy chemists' shops, we went on into an
unroofed alley, one of several which intersect the bazaar.
Here in the checkered light and shade men were busily
engaged in pounding up drugs in mortars. I took a
photo of them, and was then approached by a queer
little individual, who explained that he was a doctor and
would much like to be photographed too. Of course
all this was done through the interpreter; none of the
people spoke English.

We came out, right through the bazaar, to the other
side abutting on the river. Wide openings showed the
brilliant sunlight on the water, so strong that it made
one blink after the dimness passed through; there were
numbers of sampans and dinghies waiting at the slime-
covered steps to unload piles of shiny dark green water
melons. They would have made fine pictures, but,
alas! as so often happened, it was all "against the
sun."

The inside of the corridor or gallery seemed given up
to refreshment stalls. One very fat woman had before
her tin pans in which were diamond-shaped wedges of
rice pudding at one pice apiece—a pice equals a farthing.
We watched her for a little time and saw her serve
several customers. There was a bowl of tea, another of
hot water, and a third of milk, and she ladled some from
each impartially into a smaller bowl and with it gave to

her customer half a great cart-wheel of flat biscuit for
two pice.   At another stall the comestibles were more
savoury; there were all sorts of little dishes filled with
highly seasoned, dark coloured meats, fish, and hard-
boiled eggs cut in half; nearly everything was soaked
in curry powder and condiments.   Horrible decaying
fish formed a prominent article of diet.   Many of the
people who came to buy food were natives of India, and
it was noticeable that the things were not handed to
them in the stall-keeper's fingers, but each was allowed
to take his own; we have not arrived at so much
nicety even in our London tea-shops !

Then we passed into the fruit and vegetable market,
where on every side lay the unknown.   Great masses of
finger-like stuff resembling coral, huge bunches of
Gargantuan horse-radish, branching stalks with clusters
of green and yellow fruit like little pears from which
is made betel for chewing.   Masses of water melons
were cut open and showed such a delightful rose-pink
that I was tempted to buy one, but found the only taste
a faint flavour of holly or ivy.   A little Burmese girl
was sitting amid piles of sacks and baskets filled with a
small fruit like a little red pear; these were called rose-
apples, and she put half a dozen into my hands for a
pice, but they had less taste than a turnip.   There were
calabashes and pumpkins in plenty, and quantities of
round things about the size of potatoes, but of a lovely
plum colour; these are a vegetable named bringals,
which frequently appears at table, and rather resembles
a parsnip in taste.   There were also ladies' fingers, like
large well-developed specimens of the lords and ladies

of our childhood; as a vegetable these are very good.

The fish market produced nothing of much interest, except prawns the size of lobsters; the butcher's stall—kept by Chinese, for the Burmans would not follow such a trade—was in a corner, and then in one of the outer courts we came upon other Chinamen eating their food with chopsticks. I got a snapshot at them amid consuming laughter; they evidently considered it a tremendous joke. Some one told me that a Chinaman thinks he loses a soul every time he is photographed, but as he has seven he does not worry much about one more or less.

When I had thoroughly studied the teeming life of the bazaar I wanted to go into a choung or monastery and see what the life of the monks was like. This I did not find difficult, for the Burmans are by no means averse from strangers entering their holy precincts, though sometimes they objected to me, as a woman, going into the innermost shrine. Mah Kin Le invited us to meet her and go to a choung to see the lying-in-state of a sadaw or bishop, a very holy man, who had just died. According to custom his body, preserved in honey, would be kept for a year or more, and then burnt with great ceremony, but at the time he was merely lying-in-state in a gilt coffin. It was standing under a canopy which looked like a four-post bed and was surrounded by offerings from the faithful. In Burma the merit of the gift varies according to the sanctity of the receiver, so you gain much more by making a present to a holy man than to a beggar.

All around were many gaudy parasols with little bits of tinsel hanging from them ; the canopy was covered with silk of different colours, and as the pillars of the room were made of mirror-mosaic, the general effect was as unlike a European idea of a chamber of mourning as it well could be.   A table covered with lamps stood at the foot of the canopy, for lamps rival clocks as appropriate offerings to the poongyis.   On the verandah outside Chinese lanterns swung in the wind.   The poongyis, of whom there were several in attendance, made no objection to my taking a photograph of the scene, and two of them even stood obligingly in the foreground.   I was told on good authority that the poongyis of Burma have a high reputation, and keep their vows, but I was not personally prepossessed by their appearance ; it seems impossible that their easy idle life can be conducive to the growth of morality. They have strict rules, such as not eating after midday and not receiving money ; among other things they are not supposed to look at a woman, and the large palm-leaf fans they are frequently seen carrying are not, as might be supposed, to shield their shaven heads from the sun, but to hold up when a woman passes so as to shield them from the too dazzling effects of her beauty.

"The Book of the Law says that, even if a poongyi's mother should fall in the ditch he must not give her his hand to pull her out.   He may hold out a stick or let her seize the hem of his robe—and even then he must figure to himself that he is pulling at a log of wood."*

The poongyis do no work, but sally forth each morn-

* " Burma, a Handbook," by Sir J. G. Scott, K.C.I.E.

ing with their begging bowls, as a matter of form, to receive the offerings of the faithful; very often they are accompanied by a little neophyte whom I have seen staggering under the weight of two heavy bowls filled with food slung at each end of a bamboo, while the poongyi himself stalked serenely ahead.

A great many of the Burmese boys are still educated in the choungs, learning to read and write Burmese and to understand the simplest elements of arithmetic, and a knowledge of the Buddhist law; this is about all they do learn, and it is taught in a curious mechanical way, by the little pupils lying full length on their stomachs and repeating in a loud sing-song the Burmese characters written for them on steatite slates with sharp styles. But in places like Moulmein, where there are very large English schools, by far the greater number of boys prefer to be educated in them, for here they can learn enough to be clerks in government service. One day I wandered by myself into the mission schools of the S.P.G., the third largest in the town, containing 800 boys or more, whose fathers are in a good position and pay for their admission, but there are only a very few girls, as in spite of the very favourable position of women in Burma, and their business capacities, education is still considered unnecessary for them.

I saw both the boys and the girls playing in their respective parts of the grounds; the former to our thinking look very like girls with their funny little top-knots of hair. Numbers of the boys now, however, adopt the European fashion, and crop their hair even though they retain the lyungi. It seems almost as if

Eastern men felt that trousers are not seemly, for I
several times saw better class natives wearing trousers
with a piece of material swathed round them, and one
man had on a pair of tweed trousers and a heavy piece
of tweed cloth folded over them, under a burning sun
with the thermometer somewhere about 100° F.! It
is the Burmese fashion that every boy should be tattooed
from the waist to below the knee as soon as ever he is able
to bear it. Up-country every Burman is so adorned, but
like many old customs this is dying out in the large towns
of the south. It is such an agonising ordeal that it can
only be done a little bit at a time and the boy is given
opium to drug him while it goes on; sometimes he
nearly dies from it. The effect, when completed, is
exactly that of a pair of skin-tight blue breeches, and
as seen among the coolies, who tuck up their lyungis
into a loin-cloth while they work, it is quite effective.

There are numbers of half-castes in the S.P.G. school
besides pure Burmans. The Burmese look down on
natives of India, yet the girls do occasionally intermarry
with them, and are glad to get a Chinese husband, for
the Chinese are frugal and much more hardworking
than the Burmans. The offspring of these marriages is
divided between the races of the parents, the girls wearing Burmese clothing and the boys Chinese. In the
school, though English is taught, the lessons are
in Burmese in the lower standards, but in the highest
standards all the lessons, except the actual Burmese
one, are given in English. There were some big fellows
in these divisions, and on the blackboard I saw fairly
advanced algebraical and mathematical problems.

SADAW LYING IN STATE, MOULMEIN

25

BURMESE GIRLS AT THE S. P. G SCHOOL
MOULMEIN

Among the scholars I noticed some with a most extra-ordinary head-dress, the hair being shaved in a great bare patch running back from the forehead over the crown like a gulf. These children I was told were Corringhees.

At Moulmein there are generally a few showers and a certain cloudiness just about Christmas, but this did not happen when I was there, and every one kept repeating what a very hot " cold weather " they were having. From 180 to 200 inches of rain fall every year in six months, and then for six months there is practically none. The rain comes so refreshingly after the hot weather that it is welcomed by the inhabitants, even though it is in too great quantity. Every ditch is filled and flows merrily, the grass springs up so that its growth can almost be seen, and the trees burst out in flower. One beautiful tree, the amherstia, takes its name from a town some miles south. It was not in flower while I was at Moulmein, but I saw it afterwards with its blossoms drooping in fiery clusters. The differences in rainfall in Burma are startling and inexplicable. Rangoon gets about 80 to 90 inches a year, while northwards is a dry zone stretching for about 150 miles; this includes Mandalay, where the average rainfall is no more than 15 inches. At one place on the southern border of the dry zone called Pyinmana, one side of the river gets 60 to 80 inches and the other only 10 to 15, and for this no reason is apparent.

Whoever knows anything about Burma has heard of the Bombay Burma Trading Corporation, which was established in the country before the English

L

annexed it.   As I was staying in the house of a
manager of the corporation, I naturally heard a good
deal about the teak and forest industry, which is of exceptional interest.   He told me that there were twenty
jungle elephants belonging to the corporation to be
seen near Moulmein. They were collected together before
being taken up country to camp, and it was a most
unusual chance to be able to see so many all at once.
I agreed readily with the suggestion that we should go
to see them, and on Sunday morning early we started.
The day was heavenly, with a vivid amber light that
made every twig stand out as if bathed in radiance,
and the air had a crystalline clearness.

We drove between lines of native huts, where numbers of the people were squatting in front combing and
cleaning each other's lank black hair.   There were men
bringing water in kerosene tins; girls with baskets of
plantains on their heads ; two men were staggering along
with a heavy jar of frothy toddy slung on a pole between them ; others were hawking about crates of cheap
English enamel goods.   Bullocks were feeding on the
seeds of the toddy palm, which looked like small turnips.
In front of some of the houses was a large carefully
sketched pattern of white chalk reaching out into the
roadway.   This was designed to " keep the devils off."

When we came to the end of the village we left the
carriage behind, for it could go no further owing to the
roughness of the roads, and we started on foot through
the paddy-fields.   The threshing of the paddy was
being carried out in a simple fashion that recalled
Biblical stories : seven bullocks marched abreast, round

and round, treading the husk with their broad hoofs. Afar off we saw the elephants, huge creatures, feeding in the fields, though, truth to tell, the stubble was scanty, and there seemed little enough for them to satisfy their capacious appetites upon. Elephants are getting scarcer in Burma yearly, and their value rises accordingly ; numbers are caught in the government keddars in the north, but out of these such a large per-centage dies that the net result is small. Breeding is slow work, inasmuch as at the best it means one cub in three years, and after its birth the mother is incapacitated for work for eighteen months. A young one does not begin work at all until he is six, and is not of full use until he reaches thirty years ; so the game is not much more profitable than that of planting trees, and is carried on mainly for the benefit of those that come after. Female elephants now fetch somewhere about three hundred pounds, and males double as much. The trained elephants are of course even more valuable, and their lives are on the average shorter than the jungle elephants'.

Elephant-stealing is one of the greatest difficulties the corporation has to contend against ; every animal is not only branded but measured on a method corresponding to the Bertillon system—girth, tusks, marks and all— and yet he frequently disappears, and is not again recog- nised. The elephants I saw were all hobbled, and one, a rogue by nature, was further tethered, and did his best to express his resentment emphatically when any one came near him. I got a good photograph of one fine female, but she, poor thing, was dead within the

week, having been stung in the foot by a snake. In
spite of his apparently tough hide an elephant is really
so sensitive that even mosquitoes annoy him. The
mahouts or oozies were a rough-looking set of men, with
rather a Mongolian cast of face, light-coloured, and
medium-sized; they belong to the race of Talaings, also
called by ethnologists Môns, who were the original
owners of the land before the Burmans drove them
further and further south; they are now only found in
small numbers.

The district manager, who was with us this morning,
was going to start off next day in charge of the
elephants and this savage crew, and convoy them up to
camp, a month's journey away. He did not know the
way, and the only guidance he had was from rough
maps made by the corporation officers themselves.
Sixty miles of the way lay in Burma, and then he
crossed over into Siam, where there were no roads at
all. He seemed to look upon the whole thing as a most
ordinary performance, but I can't say I did. He was,
of course, taking his whole outfit—bedding, tent, food,
and other necessaries—and he explained to me what a
severe blow the Chicago revelations had been to him and
his fellows, who are so largely dependent on the provisions
they carry with them. Of course they shoot what game
they can, and they occasionally get fish, but the supply
of these things is limited, and sometimes rations are very
short indeed. He told me laughingly he had tried
monkey, which was disgusting, and lived for a week on
owls!

There was nothing I enjoyed more than hearing the

26

A FEMALE ELEPHANT OF THE B. B. T.
CORPORATION

TALAINGS WITH THEIR ELEPHANT
GOADS

yarns of the B.B.T.C. men, telling of the wild life in the jungle. But it is not easy to get them to talk, for they are mostly of the type that do things and do not chatter. Yet I heard enough, by dint of adroit questions, to make me understand why they are generally so resourceful and self-reliant. This great corporation, which has done so much to open up the country and to give the natives a good impression of the white sahibs' honour, began by getting concessions from Theebaw. It is tightly hemmed in by government restrictions nowadays, overlooked by forest officers, forced to plant trees where it cuts them down, and only to cut those that are allowed, which is all no doubt very good in its way, as Burmese forests are not inexhaustible. The chief work is, of course, with the teak, that splendid wood to be found everywhere in Burma, hard and durable, with a grain like oak. It is this which makes the simple and rough dâk bungalows and circuit houses look comfortable enough, whereas, were the uncovered walls and floor of deal the effect would be much barer. The trees are girdled and felled, dragged by elephants to the creeks, and sent down by water. Every one is numbered and measured. Most of the work has to be done in the wet weather when the creeks are flooded, and the men are soaked from morning till night; as one of them expressively explained to me: " It is not only you never have a dry stitch on you, but you break through jungle where on every leaf the leeches are gaping for your blood ! " This is a touching picture, but one's sympathies rather incline to the leeches, of which only one in a million can fulfil his highest destiny !

When the country near the Salween, which ran through the wild Shan States never conquered by the Burmese, was first opened up by the corporation, there was excitement enough and to spare; even now it makes an adventurous heart pant to hear of the wonders lying hid in this immense tract. Tigers, panthers, pythons and black bears live there and flourish; and there are enormous caves into which a huge river runs and disappears. My host had taken a particular interest in this curious formation, and again and again tried to penetrate into the cave, which was full of enormous stalactites, but the torches got damp, the air foul, there were great rocks to scramble over with crevasses between, and when a stone was dropped it chinked against the sides, but was never heard to reach the bottom, so the exploring party abandoned their efforts. There are sulphur springs boiling hot, and a mud volcano, which rises up in a cone like a gigantic umbrella only at full moon, and then drops down again. Many a fool buffalo has mistaken it for a mud wallow, and never been seen again. On the same great plateau there are heard strange rumblings and noises below the surface as if immense blocks of stone dropped down for ever; the natives aver the place is haunted, and will not go there, and when two Englishmen tried to sleep here they lay awake all night and in the morning with one consent fled, filled with an uncanny feeling they were loth to explain even to each other.

The thing which most surprised me in this account of jungle life was the fact that the forest managers seldom ride on the elephants : they use them for transport only, and themselves stalk ahead gun on shoulder ready to shoot at anything that presents itself. The march is very slow, about twelve or fourteen miles a day, and through thick jungle much less. I could quite realise from their word-painting how delightful it was to have outstripped your elephants on the day's march and reached a place for camp, weary and worn and soaking, with maybe your last cheroot in your pocket, and the knowledge that you may have to remain without bed or fire or food all night ; the agonising indecision as to whether you shall drag yourself back to meet the transport, or if by so doing you will run more chance of missing them, and the joy that fills your soul when the faint, far-off tinkle of the elephant bells warns you they are approaching. On the march one great source of trouble is the difficulty of inducing the elephants to cross rivers, at times they will go all right, at other times solidly refuse, and as much as a fortnight or three weeks may be wasted on the banks. There are several recognised methods of dealing with this phase of obstinacy, the animals may be driven forward with torches at night, or towed across by the corporation launch, or, if the river is rising, they may be induced to walk on to a large flat raft, where they can be fastened until the water comes up and floats them off, but all these methods involve loss of time and infinite patience.

The forest work continues right round the year except for a few months in summer. The Burmans are wonderful men with an axe, using a small narrow one like a chisel; but they are so absolutely accurate in their blows that they fell a tree very quickly, leaving the stump as smooth as a table, However, on the other hand, they are not much use at creek work, and have no sense in a jamb. A few of the best elephants trained for forest work are perfectly marvellous in their human sagacity. They will work by themselves for a long time without supervision in the river bed, feeling a jammed posse of logs with their trunks, touching this one and that one, and at length getting hold of one which they know by instinct is the keystone of the mass; they pull it out and fly for their lives to the banks, and down comes the whole avalanche of mighty tree trunks. Sometimes when the logs have collected in thousands, the dense black clouds northward bespeak rain, and a freshet is expected; this frequently happens at night, but tired or not the men must be up and about, torches are lit, and all night long the weary work goes on. The chief nuisance at these times is the plague of bugs and beetles of all sorts that swarm around the lights; every winged thing from mosquitoes upward hangs in thick black curtains around heads and torches, and they must be beaten off with the hands. Indeed, it is the small fry that render life in the jungle at times almost unendurable; besides the flying insects there are the ticks, little pinheads that attach themselves to the skin in hundreds and dig inwards, for this reason each man carries with him a square bit of Willesden canvas to sit down upon. Another great annoyance is the large hairy caterpillar, infinitely more poisonous and irritating than the creature we know.

NATIVE HOUSE

S. H. Reynolds

WOOD-CARVING ON A CHOUNG

PLATFORM OF CHUNZÔN PAGODA

WOMEN AND BABIES AT CHONZÖN

His favourite game is to crawl along a man's collar, the man rubs back, bestrewing himself unconsciously with a myriad irritable hairs; the same thing happens on the other side, at last he grabs upwards, getting the palm of his hand likewise covered with hairs, and finds that, for the hundredth time, he has fallen a victim to the hairy caterpillar. In about a quarter of an hour he begins to feel the effects of the encounter, and for days afterwards his neck is raw and painful.

In the jungle the B.B.T.C. men wear wide silk trousers and loose coats Chinese fashion, so that their clothes do not protect them much from these pests. Bees are always very troublesome, and seem to have a particular antipathy to elephants, for when they hear the elephant bells they will sometimes descend from the trees in a swarm, then the poor beasts, maddened by the stings planted in the hundreds of tender joints in their hides, fly trumpeting in every direction, and it is sometimes days before they can be got together again. One trip my host had a lively time from this cause. He was a little way from his elephants and heard them trumpet and stampede, and he dashed up a dry creek in time to run right into an angry swarm of bees. There was but little water in the creek, yet he made for a two-foot pool and lay in it even to the tip of his nose. When, after holding his breath until he was almost suffocated, he ventured to raise his head, he found the whole surface of the pool covered with floating drowning bees. He was penetrated all over with stings from head to foot, his whole body swelled up, and in the forearm alone he counted seventeen.

M

The same trip he was going along a narrow ledge between a cliff and a precipice, with the elephants in front, when he was attacked by wasps, and finally he ran his head into a red ant's nest. Red ants get their nippers buried deep, and must be detached one by one. Who would be a B.B. ?

CHAPTER V

BUDDHAS AND BATS

In England, where one day might be June and the next November, it is impossible to arrange plans for outdoor expeditions with any certainty of being able to carry them out. Things are better managed in Burma; any day may be fixed upon with the perfect assurance of fine weather. We took full advantage of this while I was at Moulmein, and of the numerous excursions planned we did not fail to enjoy every one. The most interesting of all of these was the visit to the famous Farm Caves, which lie about eight miles from Moulmein, across the river Ataran. The caves are so-called because at one time they were farmed out by the government for the sake of the rich guano with which the floor is inches deep from the presence of myriads of bats; this somewhat curious lease is now discontinued.

We were a party of four that day, and we drove the first four miles in the carriage down to the ferry over the river, followed by the servants and provisions in a gharry. At the ferry we struck upon a large party of about twenty people, Chinese husbands and Burmese wives, with their mothers and children, going also on a

pleasant outing. It is impossible to describe the
swagger of the young husbands, who looked mere lads
of about eighteen or twenty; they were as thin as
laths, a thinness accentuated by the long lean pigtails
tied up with scarlet which hung down their backs.
They wore the flopping loose Chinese raiment of a
beautiful sky-blue, huge very new leather belts full of
jewellery, gold watch chains and baubles, English sailor
straw hats, and English yellow leather lace-up shoes.
One little boy about four years old was a complete
miniature of his father : his long pigtail was elaborately
intertwined with pink, and he wore brown English
shoes ; he was evidently a great pet and was privileged
to walk ahead with the men, who sometimes carried
him for a short distance, while the whole crowd of
mothers and wives, looking extremely happy, carrying
innumerable babies and chattering like monkeys, followed their lords.   On the other side of the river amid
the brilliant green of the flat plantain leaves and the
tall spiky toddy palms were numbers of native huts, a
regular village ; when we landed we found that the
bullock carts which had been ordered for us were in
festal array, having red awnings tied to four slight uprights at the corners and gaily fluttering in the breeze.
The floor of the carts was thickly covered with straw
and the result was not at all uncomfortable.   We went
two in each cart, and so had room to move about and
change our position, but the whole of the other party,
with the exception of one man, packed into two somewhat similar carts, and seemed to enjoy the process
immensely.   The exception rode a brand-new bicycle,

and tucked one end of his pigtail into his coat pocket to prevent its interfering with him. When a Chinaman is working or travelling he generally coils his pigtail round and round the crown of his head, but it is not considered polite to leave it so in company; it would be as discourteous for a Chinaman to come up your stairs with a coiled-up pigtail as for a Burman to do so in shoes.

The road was made of laterite, as so many of the Burmese roads are, and the red dust rose a good deal too freely for comfort. The way was lined at first by bamboos and then by hedges of shiny-leaved plants like our burberous or laurel, afterwards we came to a long raised causeway running across the flat baked mud of the paddy-fields and lined by tall toddy palms. The yellow of the reaped fields and the intense blue of the hills made my eyes ache. At the corners of the fields little white flags, fluttering over huts, denoted the occupation of the broker for the purposes of selling the crop. A man was collecting toddy from the wayside palms, mounting the trees by a bamboo ladder. He makes a gash at the tough stems of the great leaves and fixes thereon a little black iron pot; the sap slowly drops into it, and he comes again some time later to collect it. As there were several pots on one tree they looked rather like some gigantic fruit. The toddy when first collected is sweet and insipid and uninteresting, but is not intoxicating. Once I had a desire to try it, and signed to a man who was coming down from a tree to give me some, he offered me an iron pot willingly enough, but when I saw the loathsome mixture of dead and dying flies floating in a scum on the surface I declined his generosity.

In front of us, gradually growing nearer, was the razor edge of the great rock I had seen from the ridge afar off. The precipitous face is scarred and seamed, showing through between skinny skeleton trunks, the very ghosts of trees. It was sheer 400 feet high and there was no place for a path on either side; it would be necessarily a hand and knee climb from base to summit, an impregnable fort of nature's construction. On the edge of the dizzy height was perched a tiny pagoda, near which we could just make out the little figure of the poongyi or hermit in charge, all alone in that tremendous glare; overhead, like a speck in the brazen sky, hovered a vulture. A more impressive sight I have rarely seen. The poongyi had no shelter from the noonday heat but the shadow of his pagoda; he was lifted far above the world and apparently inaccessible. Yet I am told that at certain festival seasons the rock is alive with good pilgrims climbing up like monkeys.

The single telegraph wire which had so far accompanied us suddenly ran off across the fields "to Siam," and we, turning a right angle, soon pulled up at the zeyats. Luckily there were two or three of these so we had not to amalgamate parties! The orientals took one and we another, which faced each other across the road. The behaviour of the whole party was excellent from beginning to end: there was none of the horse-play and skylarking English " 'Arries" would have indulged in, though continual merriment was kept up. We were amused to see all the superficial finery disappear, and then the women cooked the men's food while the men lounged about. Afterwards they waited in the background and took what their lords and masters had left. It often occurred to me in Burma how very difficult it must be for native servants to learn to attend first to their mem-sahibs before the sahibs, a custom differing so entirely from all their own. I am afraid they must think the sahibs great fools to allow such a perversion of the natural order of things!

As it is a merit to build a rest-house, but no merit to keep one in repair, they often fall to pieces. However, the one we had was perfectly clean, certainly far cleaner than it would have been in any European country. It was not unlike those I had seen at the burial-ground, a long, low, shed-like building, raised about four feet from the ground; the floor was made of boards so loosely laid together that one could easily see between. Two large gaunt pariah dogs wandered about below to pick up any scraps that might come through to them. The roof was tiled and supported by wooden posts. The ends of the shed were filled in, but the sides, the length of the building, were open, but for a light balustrade of wood, doubtless designed to keep out those same dogs at night. Part of the floor was about a foot lower than the rest making a kind of dais or edge, on which we sat while we enjoyed the breakfast the servants had cleverly prepared in an adjoining shed, There was no furniture whatever except a great earthen-ware chatty of water in which we washed our hands. Of course if one had one's own bedding the resthouse would be quite sufficient to sleep in, for in this climate at the dry season very little shelter is requisite, but all necessaries would have to be brought by the traveller.

The mighty cliff rising right opposite to us showed several yawning gaps which were the entrances to the vast caves with which it is honeycombed. In one was a little wooden bedstead and some iron pots belonging to a hermit who lived there. It seemed odd to see this evidence of domesticity in the entrance of the cave, and near it was a kind of baby pagoda perched on a shelf of rock. I can imagine the utter stillness and loneliness of the place as the poongyi prepared to settle in for the night with only the great stars blinking down on him from overhead and the occasional howl of a hungry pariah dog for company. The larger entrance led by a flight of steps to a kind of high gallery, which ran into the rock for about a hundred yards and had various caves branching from it. The main alley was lined with colossal Buddhas seated for the most part side by side. They looked ghostly in the dim light, and there was something monstrous and inhuman in the repetition of them, so still and silent, one after another. As our eyes grew accustomed to the dimness we could see that they had all different expressions: one seemed to be suffering from the colic, another was sly, a third smirking, and one seemed to say: " You may look at me, but you won't get much change out of me ! " This diversity of expression in these hand-made images was a source of continual amusement to me. Alas ! when the brass machine-made masks become common, all alike will be of a stereotyped dreariness ! Seated in front of

F. MacGeorge

THE FARM CAVES, NEAR MOULMEIN

S. H. Reynolds

BIG BELL IN THE SHWE DAGÔN
PAGODA

one image were two small carved figures of "disciples." Anything more ridiculously cheeky than their expressions I never saw, but I suppose the artist had laboured to get quite a contrary effect.

After all the most impressive thing about that cave was the smell of bat ; it was my first introduction to it, so I suppose I, like Mrs. Gummidge, felt it more than the others. It was pungent, penetrating, unforgettable ; in fact except for some " stink poochies," whose acquaintance I made later in Ceylon, I do not think I have ever met any smell which made such a deep impression on me ! How the poongyi could sleep in it—but then we do not all feel alike ; perhaps he looked upon it as a kind of company !

While I was adjusting my camera on a carefully built-up pile of wood and stone to get an exposure the whole crowd of little people in the other party streamed up the rough-hewn steps to the entrance. It was like a scene in a pantomime ; the brilliant pinks and yellows were set off to advantage by the Chinese blue ; how often have I blessed the Chinaman for giving just that colour-note the crowd needed, and which one found in nothing else. They were full of chatter and merriment, and the younger boys were screaming to imitate monkeys. They passed by into the inner recesses, and I waited till they returned, and tried to get a photo of them with a background of Buddhas ; the contrast between colossal solemnity and doll-like daintiness would have been striking. Unfortunately, the older women when they saw my intention held their noses and ran ; I do not know if they attributed to my

N

camera what by strict rights appertained to the bats, but it seemed so. One Chinaman swaggered up to us and said grandly: "Too much afraid; they not understand!"; but he did not offer to pose himself, in spite of his superior wisdom.

On leaving this cave we walked for about a quarter of a mile in the deep shade of the perpendicular cliff that almost made one giddy to look up at it, and then finally mounted to the second entrance by a narrow path, winding upward through jungle flower growing shoulder high. I had never been in a stalactite cave before, and expected frosty pinnacles and hanging spikes of a snowy whiteness; in this I was disappointed; when our eyes grew accustomed to the dim light that fell through irregular shafts and air-holes we saw strange pale colours, greens and yellows, but no snowy whiteness. Then one of our party arranged and lit a flare of magnesium powder, and the effect was wonderful. Over the high arched roof the bats flew screeching in countless multitudes. In the centre was one huge cluster like a swarm of bees, and from this continuous flights of them radiated so fast across the roof that it made one's eyes run to watch them. We set off the powder several times, and at the last the party of little people from the first cave came in time to see it, and were struck dumb with admiration and awe. By this light we saw better the various forms of the rocks, which were fantastic and peculiar; there were some like filmy shawls, others like mammoth elephants, and others resembling cathedral columns, but all appeared as if draped and softened by some covering of gauze. Here and there columns of

stalagmite rose from the floor, and the roof was honey-
.combed with deep pits or cauldrons. We were not
satisfied with staying near the entrance, but, in spite of
an ever-deepening sense of the presence of our friends the
bats, scrambled on over rough rocks for a considerable
distance until we could penetrate no further. Insensibly
we had become so much accustomed to the cooler air in
the cavern that when we emerged once more, the
warmth outside, even in the shade, struck our faces like
the blast from a furnace.

On arriving again at the rest-house we found the
servants had prepared tea, and afterwards, in the cool of
the evening, we started homeward. The only incident
on the return journey had its comic side. As we neared
the ferry Mr. M. told me that a Burman, whom he
knew, or whose aunt or grandmother he knew, in the
way of business, had asked us to come into his house in
passing and he had pleaded lack of time, but promised
that we should speak to him on our return. He was
there, evidently expecting us, and as we alighted from
our lordly waggons he set out a small round table in the
middle of the dusty village street and put round it four
chairs for us to sit down upon. Then he brought out a
magnificent worked silver bowl of huge size, covered
with a plate. All around us, in awed delight, stood the
village population, mostly consisting of children; I do
not think I ever saw so many children, or children quite
so naked, all in one place at one time before or since.
Two tumblers were placed on the table; it was intended
that we should drink after the men, of course, and when,
with immense solemnity, the plate was removed, the

bowl was discovered to be full of plain water, none too cold! I thought this might have been meant as an insult, but I was assured that that was quite out of the question where a Burman was concerned; it was, probably, all the man had to offer. If he had offered the bowl as well there might have been something to say for it! However, we braved typhoid, and sipped a little of the water so as not to hurt our entertainer's feelings.

The Farm Caves was only one among a number of excursions.

Another day we went by small launch down the river to Chonzôn (pronounced Chonzone), a trip which can be done equally well by taking the regular steamer of the Flotilla Company. We started from Tiger jetty about 8 A.M., and in the golden morning light dropped down the broad stream with the tide. There was a slight blue haze in the air which seemed to envelop everything as in a veil of shining gauze, and made the low-lying green scrub on the far side of the river the colour of aloes. On the hills around Moulmein the little pagodas shone as points of dazzling whiteness, and the broad band of silver on the large one sparkled like diamonds. The paddy-boats with their red brown sails, the Chittagonian boats with high sterns like gondolas, and the Burmese boats with their hoods, were each and all a source of delight.

It seemed a blissful idea to travel down-stream for many days in one of the last, with the thatch beehive roof to shield one from the sun, but I am told that the reality is anything but blissful. The thatch covering is too low to permit of any one's standing up, or even sitting with much comfort. Lying down full length gets fatiguing after a time, besides, it is impossible to see anything in that position ; yet it is imperative to remain under the shelter while the sun is high. The squeak of the oars—in which the boatman delights as much as the cartman does in his ungreased axles—gets perfectly maddening after a while. At night the boat-men talk incessantly, and are offensive in their habits, so the joys of coming down-stream in a native boat are more than counterbalanced by the evils.

We landed at last amid a many-coloured crowd on a wooden jetty, and passed beneath overhanging tassels of bright scarlet hybiscus to where a motley collection of carts awaited our choice. Then came a long dusty drive through paddy-fields lined by small wild pumpkin trees laden with fruit like green apples. Presently we arrived at the bungalow and court-house, where our host for the day welcomed us. After lunch I and a friend wandered up to the high pagoda, about half a mile away. A long flight of steps led up to it as usual, and at the base were two fine specimens of the leogryphs generally seen in this position ; their eyes were of the transparent red tinsel or glass that has a ferocious gleam in the sunlight.

From the pagoda platform there was a wide and beautiful view. We sat there a long time having a glimpse of the glittering sea on the far horizon, and noting the splendid butterflies, some the size of small birds, that fluttered past. There was a large plaster elephant on one side of the pagoda platform, an offering from some wealthy Burman. The white elephant is a sacred animal, and is often represented in carvings at pagodas, but it was odd to see one alone like this and so singularly placed.

Later on, when it was cooler, we went down to the village on the shores of a wide shallow lake. Here the camera created great excitement. Though the light was going, and the trees threw heavy shadows, I tried to get a group of the people to pose, and just as I was about to take them, a woman rushed wildly up and squatted down in front. The minute the photo was taken there was a universal roar of laughter from the good-natured villagers. I failed to see the joke, but it was evidently a good one, for they laughed and laughed consumedly, and passed it on from one to another as if it were too good to waste. Just then my host came up and explained that it was because the woman, who ran up at the eleventh hour, had been bathing, and had only her bathing lyungi on, and no little white engie or jacket; but she had been so anxious not to be left out that she had plumped down just as she was. Even after we left the village the laughter still went on, ringing up the aisles of the heavy-foliaged trees. Judging by the way it was received jokes must be scarce in Chonzôn; I should not be surprised if this one turns up in the Christmas number of the next " Chonzôn Gazette," or whatever the equivalent may be. As we turned away an excited group hurried after us, and by signs made known that they wished to extract the photo from the camera; my attempts to explain that the feat was impossible were in vain, until one more learned in the

ways of cameras than the others came along. He stood
in front of me majestically, and pointed with both hands
to the sun, and then to me, and then to the camera, and
what he said I know not, but the others understood and
dispersed.

This village was very pretty and very irregular; all
the little huts stood on legs, as they invariably do, a
fact which adds a piquant touch to an eye unaccustomed
to it. There were many fine trees overshadowing them,
amongst which I recognised that bearing the jack-fruit,
a large green pumpkin with prickles, which grows on a
stalk straight out of the trunk in a most surprising way.
It is uninteresting to eat, and only used by the poorest.
I tried to get views of this fascinating village from the
lake, where a number of boys were bathing joyously,
but the evening light failed me.

The life of a Burmese villager is a very happy one,
paddy is cheap, and rice forms the staple of his diet; he
generally has a growth of papyas or plantains for his
household use. A papya is a large fruit like a melon,
only pear-shaped. Inside it is a rich yellow colour, and
the hollow centre is filled with seeds like peppercorns.
The usual way to eat the fruit is with a dash of lime and
some sugar; but a friend I saw in Ceylon—where they
are just as common, but are called papaws—told me the
true method was to have it in a finger-bowl with sherry
and cream, and having tried it I can truly say it is
excellent. Clothing need trouble the Burman villager
little; he can get enough stuff for a lyungi for a rupee,
if he ever goes to the mad extravagance of buying one.
Judging by those I saw, I should think they were

generally family heirlooms, having been washed and
worn until they had long lost all semblance of their
first colour.   Children need no clothes at all ; the few
bangles and beads distributed among them are doubtless
family capital.   I always found these little mites very
attractive, they seemed so happy, and when they smiled
they looked all teeth and bright dark eyes.   They were
sometimes, but not often, afraid of me, and when they
were it was generally in a coy way that added to their
charm, making them bury their faces in their mothers'
engies and peep out to see if I were watching them.
The men are as a rule kind and contented ; the prevailing disposition is one of good fellowship, and there seem
to be hardly any beggars.   In the rainy season, of course,
the thatch and mat huts must be penetrated through
and through by the damp, and the whole place is a
swamp, but it is not cold driving rain as it would be with
us, and where you have nothing to spoil there is no
reason to be anxious.   To compare this life, without
care, and full of good fellowship and affection and plenty,
with that of an East-end dweller who works for a
pittance in a foul den, is to compare heaven with
hell.

Another day we went from Moulmein up the river
to a very pretty village at Kado.   The launch took us
this time also, and we passed within sight of Martaban
on the other shore.   I wished I could have gone further
northward from here to one of the most famous of the
Burmese pagodas, Chaik-To, which stands on a boulder
looking as if a finger touch would send it crashing
down, but this expedition would have taken many days,

VILLAGERS AT CHONZÒN

KADO, A MODEL VILLAGE

and I, who had so much else to see, could not spare the time.

We passed for some distance close along by the shore, where the silvery leaves of the gangall, turning their cottony backs to the wind, looked exactly like those of willows. The untidy heads of the areca palm, the green of the flat plantain leaves, and the tall elephant grass were all mingled in confusion. Everything was so beautiful and we went so smoothly that it seemed all care was left behind. It came as a slight chill to find that the basket of food we had brought had to be suspended from the roof of the launch to prevent the intrusion of the white ants !

As we neared Kado sampans came out to land us, for we could not get near to the landing-stage owing to the shallowness of the water. The way in which a native uses his oars in a sampan is very graceful, and like many another thing looks very easy until you try. He stands upright and crosses the tops of the oars, working them backwards entirely by a wrist movement. It is curious that the boats, both large and small, should so resemble the boats at Venice. In the evenings, when seen against the yellow glow, a large Chittagonian boat seems as if cut out in black velvet, and the effect is almost exactly that of a gondola, even to the action of the gondolier; and I believe that sampans are actually identical with those used at Venice.

The village at Kado was quite a model one; there was a long raised causeway down the centre of each street, and the huts stood on legs on both sides. In the wet weather the whole place is under water. Sticking

o

out of the thatch of the houses were strange-looking
implements ; they consisted of a rough hook on the end
of a tall bamboo and a primitive looking flat fan, also
on a bamboo handle.   These things are put there by order
for the purpose of tearing down the thatch and beating
out the flames if a hut catches fire, and stowed away
in the rafters every villager must keep two chatties
full of water in view of the same catastrophe.   Pariah
puppies swarmed, for, owing to his horror of taking life,
the Burman never kills the superfluous members of a
litter, and consequently a poor lean mangy mother,
with a family of seven or eight miserable little specimens of unwanted life clinging to her who has little
support to give them, is a frequent sight.   In the
village there were many flowers, one a very pretty bell-
shaped, sulphur-yellow flower like a convolvulus, with a
deep crimson centre.   I saw this again in the jungle
near Maymyo.   Another which grew in hedges was
not unlike leopard's-bane ; it is also common in Moulmein itself.   There were pretty little acacia trees with
powdery scented white blossoms, but as a whole I was
disappointed with the flowers of the country.

Many very wealthy merchants live in this village,
which was quite the neatest and cleanest I saw during
my whole time in Burma, and they have erected some
famous modern shrines and pagodas which attract
numbers of pilgrims. · We passed on to these through
the shady enclosure of a large poongyi choung.   I could
not resist entering the choung itself and went up the
steps and into the darkness of the great hall, but I had
not advanced far when a small poongyi sprang out of

the gloom behind some columns, and waved me back.
Though he did not look very fearsome, I was yielding
to custom and retreating, when at a signal given by
Mr. M. he withdrew the heavy gold-worked curtain
suspended before the shrine so that we could see the
gilt Buddha behind. This was the only time that any
inmate of a choung objected to my going anywhere
I liked. The hall was full of offerings, lamps of every
shape and size in multitudes, and very many clocks,
some of them the large common white-faced, deal-cased
clocks to be seen hanging on any cottage wall in
England. Burmese offerings set strongly in these two
directions; it certainly does give the poongyi something to do to wind up the clocks, for they generally
seem to keep them going, but why lamps? I expect it
is the old story of "do as you would be done by," and
in the dim recesses of a cottage the Burman pictures
the glories of an oil lamp until it seems the most
beautiful thing in the world. Several offerings assumed
more original forms; one was an ordinary iron bedstead.

We presently passed on from all this display of
treasures to the new shrines behind the choung; these
were dazzlingly ornate, all gilt and mirror-mosaic with
many roofs rising high into the shining sky. Running
like a frieze round the courts are bas-reliefs and pictures
representing the tortures of hell and delights of heaven
in the crudest material manner. People being sawn in
two and burning head downwards or nipped by innumerable devils recalled the sensations with which, in
one's childhood, one looked at Dante's Inferno as illus-

trated by Doré. Hanging in front of the monstrous
Buddhas in the shrines were the little paper streamers,
to be bought everywhere for a few pice; there were
also flowers in abundance, some of the blossoms of the
frangipanni being pickled in a bottle ! But some of the
offerings were grotesquely inappropriate; one was a
screen made of the photos of actresses to be found in
cheap boxes of cigarettes, another was a pack of playing-
cards gummed together corner to corner, and a third a
representation of Mr. Chamberlain cut out in concertina
paper as sold on the London pavements. It is most
natural that what appears to the worshipper rare and
uncommon should be offered, but to Europeans the
effect is often almost paralysing. A tea-planter with
whom I stayed in Ceylon told me that his two native
servants were Roman Catholics, and they with others
built a chapel and asked him to come and see it; he
went, but could with difficulty restrain his mirth at
seeing the whole of the altar draped with copies of the
" Pink 'Un " !

In one shrine we had representations of all the
three attitudes of the Buddha, and round the walls
of the " museum " was a most extraordinary frieze,
showing natives as black men and the Burmans as
white; this frieze is considered a great joke by the
Burmans themselves, and attracts thousands on holidays.
Of course the Burmans are much fairer than the natives :
their skins are coffee or honey coloured, and they class
themselves with the white races. Colonel Yule says,
" By a curious self-delusion the Burmans would seem to
claim in theory at least they are a white people."

This was the last of that splendid series of expeditions which added so much to my time in Moulmein, for on January 2 I had to leave, to go back to Rangoon preparatory to starting off up-country alone. Much as I looked forward to this, it was a sad wrench leaving, but early as was the hour of the steamer's departure, numbers of my friends came down to " give me a send-off," and even as the boat moved slowly away I saw one topee and another being added at the last minute to the flower-bed of Oriental turbans which adorned the wharf.

CHAPTER VI

THE ROAD TO MANDALAY

THE artificial life passed amid streets, or enclosed by four walls, has a softening effect on many, who become like sea creatures without shells, flabby and unable to help themselves in the rough and tumble of the wilderness; when a breath of colder air blows upon these people they are chilled and feel awesomely alone. But there are a few not yet so sensitised by their surroundings, that they cannot pant for the outer air, blowing free and fresh, and the aloneness that comes with it, which is freshening and vitalising. However, they seldom "get out"; the ways around our towns are beaten flat by many feet for many leagues, and to go beyond is costly and difficult.

When I finally left Moulmein and Rangoon I was sorry enough to say good-bye to the "much" I had had of enjoyment and the "many" who had been good to me, but yet I felt keenly excited at the prospect of getting away quite by myself up-country to penetrate even ever so little "into the rough" on my own account.

But I was not quite alone, for I had Chinnasawmy, and he made a vast deal of difference. He had acted as second "butler" to Mrs. M. and was now leaving her, so she suggested that as he was a good boy, I should take him on. He was a Madrassee aged twenty-six, not very tall, with a round brown face and round brown eyes, and a splendid set of white even teeth which seldom showed, as his habitual expression was one of great solemnity. His wardrobe consisted of a mysterious garment called a dhoti, which was wound in and about his brown legs, a short coat of brown cloth much worn, a turban and a pair of tiny gold earrings. This was his travelling get-up, and when we were staying in the house of friends he donned a white twill or jean coat in place of the brown one, and if waiting at table, and very smart indeed, a long white one with a very broad stiff waistband. But dhobies were required if these coats were much worn, and dhobies came expensive, so the brown coat was frequently in evidence. The boy paid his own washing, though I helped him a little at the end when I insisted on his wearing the smarter uniform continuously. In addition to his own outfit, I gave him, as I understood it was proper to do if you were taking a boy into the colder country, ten rupees to buy a long coat and a rug.

I had told him at first I would give him thirty rupees a month, but he came and explained to me, very nervously, for he was a timid boy, that he would prefer it if I would give him "butter-money" daily, and less at the end of the month. I agreed to this, and arranged to pay him twenty-five rupees a month instead, and four annas a day; this came to a little more but it was really cheap for a travelling boy, and I found him well worth it. He was a very good linguist, speaking, reading and writing English, besides his own two languages, Tamil and Hindustanee. Much later, when we were crossing to Ceylon, where I took him with me, I, being an ignoramus, asked him if he spoke Tamil, thinking Hindustanee was his native language ; he said yes, so I asked if he spoke it well or only a little, and when he replied " It is mine own tongue, Missie," I felt rather small ! He also spoke Burmese quite fluently, but had forgotten how to read it ; he knew Telugu and a little French. The last accomplishment I found out by accident, for when I was at Maymyo, wishing to say something to a friend while he was in the room, I talked to her for a few minutes in French, and the same evening he remarked to me with his customary gravity, " I understand French too, Missie, well's English, but I nearly forgotten him."

This, as a delicate blend of warning for the future and saving my feelings, could hardly be bettered !

I asked him how he had learned all these languages, and he said, " English very easy, Missie ; I learned for three months with a munshi (teacher)." He had come over to Burma at the age of fourteen, and was quite alone in the world ; he told me this in answer to a question, for he very very rarely volunteered anything : " No father, no mother, Missie, no brothers or sisters ; father dead, mother dead, when him little boy of seven, no one but one friend, him chokrah to Mr. ——," and he named a man I knew in Moulmein. Of course with natives mere wives do not count, and it does not do to

CHINNASAWMY CHAFFING
COOLIE GIRLS

A VILLAGE SCENE

inquire too closely into domestic arrangements, but I have no doubt there was a wife in Moulmein.

I was so unaccustomed to native servants that at first I did not know what to do with the boy, or what to ask him to do for me, which was the more important of the two. I had heard so much about the prejudices of caste and so on, that I feared telling him to do something which he might refuse, and then I should have been in a difficulty. I was quite aware it would not do to let him see that I was anything but authoritative and self-confident, or his respect for me would have vanished, so I always pretended to know everything, and gradually grew more used to the manners and customs of the land. I must say for Chinnasawmy he did everything I told him; there was no question of caste. I was never so well looked after in my life. He was valet, interpreter, footman, cook, housemaid, and everything else combined. He called me in the morning, tidied my room whenever I came out of it, packed and unpacked, accompanied me everywhere, and as he grew to know me better his small attentions were quite touching. If I were sitting in a deck chair on the verandah he would fetch my cushion, or if I were writing on my knee without the blotting-pad he would get it; he always noticed everything. He knew all my possessions better than I did myself, and could lay his hands on the tiniest trifle. I think he was never so happy as when examining and handling my small belongings, or tidying my trunks, shaking out all the blouses and skirts! It was amusing also to notice how thoroughly he identified himself with me; he used

P

to ask : " Our jam, Missie, or derwan's jam ? " It was always " our biscuits," " our tea," though of course he did not touch these things himself. He did not give me occasion to be angry with him, though I never over-looked anything he happened to do wrongly ; but he often saw me assert myself when other natives or half-castes were not so well-mannered as they should be, and so he held me in wholesome awe.

Many people have an idea that all natives are rogues and liars, only to be terrorised or dragooned into keeping straight. This is, of course, absurd ; service won on those lines stands on a rotten foundation ; but it is certainly true that a slack, good-humoured master or mistress will not win the same devotion as one who, though kind and just, has the power of sternness. The native is child enough to want strength in his protector, he respects a master who *is* master. There is in fact a Tamil pro-verb : " A master without anger, a servant without wages." No doubt many of the natives are entirely without conscience as we consider it, but there is a small minority born faithful, and Chinna was of this class. I came across a few like him in some of the houses of my friends, and generally found that they had been with the household for twelve or fifteen years, and were trusted members of it. He was never cheeky, it was not in his nature, and he had not the awful glib superficiality of my first attendant in Rangoon. He was painstaking and sensible ; and, though I often had to repeat an order twice slowly, I knew if he said he understood I could rely on him. At the outset I told him not to be afraid to ask again if he did not understand anything, as it was better to ask than to do the thing wrong.

I took tickets through Cook for the whole of the up-country tour, including both rail and steamer for the boy and myself, and the whole cost me roughly between fourteen and fifteen pounds. This carried us up by rail to Mandalay, rail and steamer, or steamer alone, to Bhamo, and back the same way; by rail from Mandalay to Maymyo and Gokteik and back, down from Mandalay by river to Prome and from Prome by rail to Rangoon, or practically over nearly all the railways there are in the country.

We left Rangoon at midday on Monday, January 7, and I was lucky enough to get a carriage to myself. The trains in Burma are not corridor, but each first-class compartment has a lavatory attached to it. There are generally only two first-class compartments on a train, and the seats run longitudinally instead of transversely as with us. There are, high up, two other seats, which can be used as top berths at night if required. It is always well, if possible, to give notice of your intention of going, before the train starts, so that the carriage can have an extra sweeping and dusting; and this is especially the case if a lady is travelling alone at night, because by applying beforehand she can get one carriage labelled "Ladies only," which is a great boon. The Eurasians generally make for the second classes, and the natives are crammed as tightly as herrings in a barrel into the hard wooden thirds and very often locked in.

I knew I should have to spend the night on the train, and had brought with me a resai, which, to use an

Irishism, is a kind of cheap " eider-down " stuffed with cotton, a sheet, a rug, and a cushion, and I had also one of those invaluable expanding Jap baskets, containing a few things I might want. I was quite in the fashion with my basket, for they are largely used in the country, only they are generally covered with Willesden canvas to keep out the wet and the insects. As luggage is registered through, something of this kind is necessary in the carriage.

I was not even yet altogether off on my own account, for on arrival at a junction some few miles from Mandalay I intended to change and go to Sagaing, a little further down the river, there to stay for a day or so with the Commissioner and his wife, who were friends of Mrs. M.'s. The first part of the journey is very uninteresting, the line running through flat paddy-fields. with sun-baked mud and yellow stagnant pools, in which great buffaloes wallowed ; buffaloes always inspired me with loathing, they looked so unclean, like immense black pigs. Near the stations were piles of paddy-sacks waiting for transport. Soon the blue Salween hills came into sight and rather broke the monotony of the landscape, and tall grass with great feathery heads of an exquisite whiteness, like snow, grew along by the line. We passed Pegu, which was one of the places I regretted not seeing, as there are wonderful pagodas there, and some curious colossal Buddhas. From the railway one could see nothing. Pegu was the headquarters of the Talaing or Môn race suppressed by the Burmans. At about seven the train stopped at a place called Toungoo, and we were given a short half-

S. H. Reynolds

SCENE AT A RAILWAY STATION

S. H. Reynolds

MONSTER BUDDHA AT AMARAPURA

hour for dinner. This was the frontier town of the English before the Third Burmese War. The refreshment room was passable, and the food pretty fair; there were two white men dining besides myself, officers rejoining their regiments at Maymyo; I talked to one of them a little, as here where Europeans are few and far between one learns to be friendly at sight. When I returned to my carriage I found that Chinna had spread the rugs out very comfortably, making a bed on the broad seat, and had filled my aluminium tea apparatus with water to boil. Alas! I soon discovered that the hideous jolting of the train prevented any experiments in that direction.

The light was very dim in the carriage, and it was out of the question to read, but sitting there comfortably watching the great stars, which seemed twice as bright as in England, seeing the station platforms with their extraordinary assortment of natives, and knowing that one was being swiftly whirled along through a new country, were occupation of thought enough for one evening.

I did not sleep badly, though I kept waking with a start lest I should have missed the junction where I was to change. We arrived at it at about six in the morning. It was cold and very grey. As I peered out I saw the strange name Myohaung, but no sign of Chinna, whom I had told to get out and come to me. I had to go along the train calling for him, and when at last I found him he tumbled out as if he were hardly awake. There did not seem to be any sign of an official about, but there were many weird figures swathed over head and shoulders in bath towels, which seem to be the favourite wear for early morning. I told him to ask one of these whether this was the right place at which to change for Sagaing, and the figure so addressed suggested with great volubility that we should get into the train and go on to Mandalay. I patiently explained, through the boy, that we were not going to Mandalay but Sagaing : Bath-towel seemed to think that we had better change our minds and go to Mandalay after all ; apparently it was his only idea. At last, moved by a brilliant inspiration, I waved my hand to indicate the far side of the platform, and asked where the train went to that came in there. The answer being translated showed that it ran to Amarapura Shore and there stopped, and Bath-towel very urgently advised us not to try it ; but now I knew. Had not my directions told me that I must get on a steamer before reaching Sagaing ? So, in spite of much good advice, we let the Mandalay train go on without us, and prepared to camp on the cheerless platform until it should please Providence to send a train that went in the opposite direction. I sat and watched the yellow sunrise and found much to interest me in the platform itself, decorated by poongyis in their yellow robes, vendors of unwholesome sticky sweet-meats and decayed fish, and a variety of grotesquely-clad natives. One man had procured from somewhere an Inverness cape, beneath which his bare brown legs showed comically.

The boy made many friends, who helped him to carry my small impedimenta and kept up a subdued chatter, and thus an hour passed. At length the train came in, not as one might expect, at the platform, but away

across some lines.   However, I had been on the look-
out, feeling instinctively it would try to sneak away
without us if it could, so I saw through the manœuvre
and boarded it.   After a long interval we moved out of
the station, and two of the men, with whom the boy
had apparently struck up a lifelong friendship, hung on
for quite a considerable way before dropping easily off
and walking back to the platform.   The few miles
between Mandalay and Amarapura Shore are among
the most interesting I remember.   I went over them
several times again and always at a foot's pace, though
this is not a little branch, as might be supposed, but
part of the only railway route to the north.   One time
I remember there was no van, and so my large box had
to be hoisted on to the little platform outside the carriage.   It stood across the rail, and the boy held it on
all the time ; as long as we were pleased no one else
objected—it is not Germany.   The jolting was terrible,
but even had it fallen it could not have come to much
grief, as we went so slowly.   It was a scene fertile in
detail.   On the telegraph wires were little green birds
with long tails and yellow heads ; immense goats with
long flapping ears browsed about the rails and moved
away as we crawled up to them ; numbers of worn grey
pagodas crumbling into ruin stood in melancholy groves
on each side ; fascinating little thatch and mat huts
with deep brown shadows in their depths stood on legs,
and beneath them rolled children and pariah dogs.   The
rich greens of the fresh plantain leaves made vivid colour
patches, and here and there was a sudden flash of richest
rose, and behold a web of silk of some twenty feet in

length stretched on a loom, with a woman working at it by hand.

Amarapura was the capital of the country before the uprising of Mandalay, and beyond it is another ancient capital, Ava, from which the court took its name.   Soon we came in sight of the Sagaing hills across the river, wrinkled in innumerable folds and holding in every fold a small pagoda, which gleamed white in the now steady sunlight.   We crept along to Amarapura Shore, and stopped on the very edge of the river looking down a cliff-like bank of sand, beneath which lay a large steamer.   Here every one got out, and I did the same.   I struggled down the soft sliding sand and crossed the gangway in safety.   On the steamer forward I found a pleasant deck and was glad to get tea and toast and marmalade, for I was very hungry.

We remained where we were for perhaps forty minutes, then slowly moved out across the river and stopped at the other side.   The whole scene was alive with movement; I saw gay little sampans carrying brightly-dressed passengers; on shore a man wrestled with two little Burmese ponies gorgeous in tasselled harness; it was all very bright and very clear.   I sat still drinking it in and enjoying myself immensely, until it occurred to me we had waited there a very long time. When were we going on to Sagaing? I asked a native who hovered about and had apparently something to do with the boat, and he said this was Sagaing; it had not occurred to me, certainly, that such a large steamer was employed simply in going backwards and forwards across a not very wide river !

STATION AT AMARAPURA SHORE

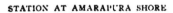

SAGAING SHORE

I struggled up another long and sandy bank in the
heat, which was now great, and at the top, near the
station, found a dog-cart waiting; a few minutes later
my host and hostess came up on horseback. I had not
met them before, but when one is the only European on
train or steamer, as so often happens here, there is not
the same difficulty of identification as there might be,
say, at Waterloo.

We drove back along the margin of the river to the
bungalow. Sagaing is one of the prettiest places in
Burma. It is overshadowed by huge tamarinds, which
have a leaf something like an acacia, and combine shade
and grace inimitably. A bund runs along by the river,
and in the dry season, as when I was there, a stretch of
grass lies below reaching down to long sandbanks, but
in the wet season the water comes right up to the
bund. The bungalow is built on the very edge of the
bund and, surrounded by charming flowers and shrubs,
is a very model of homely comfort; poinsettias, startling
in their glory, twice the height of a man, masses of
bougainvillea and beautiful broad-leaved plants, green
and gold, without number surrounded it.

Though Sagaing seems so peaceful from the banks of
the river, it is a busy place, where the making of earthen-
ware pots and brass bowls is carried on to a large
extent. During the two days I stayed there I saw
many interesting sights. Huge ruined pagodas of red
and yellow brick, falling into decay by the roadside,
overgrown with shrubs and creepers, majestic in their
utter desolation, others new and in good preservation—
at one a tiny boy was being taught by two women to

hold up an offering of food toward the shrine; another, bell-shaped and startlingly white, is very conspicuous from a long distance round. One afternoon we rode to the foot of the Sagaing hills. It was years since I had been on horseback, and I felt considerable qualms in anticipation; but the pony—he was only thirteen hands one—who carried me behaved well, and, after all, it was mostly walking, for the roads were just dried water-courses, full of great lumps and depressions. At the base of the hills we left the ponies with the syces and ascended by a broad red-brick causeway, very broken and ruinous. Though it was after four o'clock the sun was still very hot, and there were everywhere scrubby bushes of very catchy thorns that made walking a difficulty. On one side of the hill we came to the " Thirty Caves," an arcade with thirty openings. It is partly cut out of the rock and partly artificial. Inside are seated forty-five Buddhas, supposed to be exactly alike; they are of plaster, painted, and by no means beautiful. We adorned the neck of one with my puggaree, which had been torn from my head by a high-growing thorn-tree while I was riding, and it was impossible not to imagine a smile of grim satisfaction on his face, while those on each side seemed perceptibly sulkier. I am sure if one watched an image of the Buddha long enough one could imagine it moved. Then we descended into the strangest nook—a broad court in a niche of the hillside, with choungs and pagodas around it, and an evil-looking tank loathsome with green slime; in the courtyard were several trees, including the sweet flowers of jasmine and rose. The yellow sunlight lay peacefully on the hill,

but here was all dark shadow and it was very quiet;
we only saw one old woman. Then we walked along
the summit of the ridge on a flagged causeway. We
climbed at last, after looking down on numerous
pagodas, to the highest part of the ridge where is the
largest of all, and here we waited to see the sun set.
The river makes a great elbow, almost a right angle,
round the hill, and can be seen on both sides. As the
sun fell the hills became amethyst and the river pale
green.

The intense quietness and stillness sank like dew into
my Londoner's soul. The sounds that were heard were
only sufficient to call attention to the quality of stillness
that was in the air. The shrill scream of a jungle-cock,
the gentle cooing of a wood-pigeon, a murmur of soft
voices rising up the hillside, and now and again the
tinkle of one silver-toned bell from the htee of the
pagoda. Near by was a frangipanni-tree, with its sweet
white blossoms scenting the air. The sun, huge in
diameter, touched the edge of the horizon, where it was
as flat as the sea, and seemed to drop behind it all at
once. There followed a magnificent lingering red-gold
glow, broken up by the wedge-shaped streamers I have
never seen in England.

At this spot, watching another sunset, stood Colonel
Yule, in 1855, with the other members of the mission
sent to King Mindon Min at Amarapura. Yule says:
" Nothing on the Rhine could be compared to it." A
little further on he states : " It might have been Venice,
it looked so beautiful." And again : " Our impression
was that the Lake of Como could not be finer, and those

who had seen Como said it was not." Truly the scene lost nothing by the variety of his comparisons ! To me it was just Burma, and not in the least like any European country.

We wandered down another broken red causeway with jagged uneven steps, and at the foot met the ponies which the syces had brought along, and so home in the evening air.

I found it impossible to "do" Mandalay, as I had hoped, from Sagaing. Though only ten miles distant the train takes an interminable time, and the last one leaves Mandalay at three in the afternoon, after which comes the best part of the day; so reluctantly I took farewell of my kind hosts, and, carrying with me ineffaceable memories of beautiful Sagaing, went into Mandalay.

CHAPTER VII

THE GOLDEN CITY

My first vision of Mandalay, the Golden City, was not an inspiring one. The train got in about midday, and I looked out upon a good-sized station, and a strong fence guarded by a ticket-collector, behind whom appeared the motliest throng I had yet seen. I did not know there was another exit for the first-class passengers, and so I meekly followed my luggage as it was carried out to the gharries through this thronging crowd. I knew better another time. As the box and the gharry were about the same size, there was some difficulty in fitting the one on to the other, but it was done. I squeezed inside into the very small space that the remainder of my possessions left for me, and looked on with amusement while poor Chinnasawmy, with the expression of an old sheep amid a pack of ravening wolves, attempted to satisfy the demands of those who thronged upon him for backsheesh in compensation for their share in lifting the said box to its perilous position.

When we finally got away from their clamour and on to the road outside, I was surprised to see tram-lines; an electric car runs right down to the shore of the river, about three miles away. It is a great boon, as it goes much more quickly and smoothly than a gharry, and the front part is reserved for first-class passengers. Very near the station is the dâk bungalow, standing in a dusty compound. I had not then tried the delights of a dâk bungalow, but was destined to have that gap in my experience amply filled.

The address I had given to the gharry wallah was that of Gales's hotel, for though I had been preceded at Mandalay by a note of introduction to the Deputy-Commissioner, I had learned from my friends at Sagaing he was much harassed on account of an outbreak of plague, and I did not want to bother him further. Also, in my innocence, I fancied the hotel would do very well. There is besides the hotel in Mandalay a boarding-house and circuit house, as well as the dâk bungalow. An ordinary visitor must try for accommodation at the first two before he can be admitted to the third, unless he has a letter of introduction from the Deputy-Commissioner. As for the circuit house, that is a very superior place indeed, reserved for Government and other officials.

The road from the station comes out on one side of the moat which lies four-square in the town, enclosing the old red wall of the palace. Along this we passed, and down another side, before turning into the town proper, where there were wide streets of whitewashed and other buildings, some substantial and some untidy, but all lacking any sort of interest or beauty.

Externally the hotel did not look unprepossessing, but internally ——

I was told there was only one room vacant, and that

was on the ground floor. I was led to it through the principal eating-room, where several English people were having tiffin. On the raising of a dirty curtain I saw the filthiest room it has ever been my lot to enter: the stained, discoloured walls had once been white-washed; the mattresses that lay uncovered on two rickety wooden bedsteads effloresced a strong odour; there was plenty of evidence of other occupants of an indescribable nature. From one side of the room opened off a noisome cupboard, absolutely dark, and about the size of a large hearthrug. This was the bath-room! I stepped across and looked out of the window into a pestilential back-yard surrounded by high walls. For this accommodation the native in charge demanded eight rupees a night! I wondered what I looked like, and would have glanced at the glass had there been such a thing. Evidently my month in the East had not rubbed off the European bloom to any great extent. It was the work of a few minutes to get out a sheet of note-paper and write a note adding to the worries of the Deputy-Commissioner by asking him to tell me of any accommodation—clean—where I could lodge. Then I left my luggage at the hotel for the while and drove back all along the side of the moat to the Deputy-Com-missioner's house, which lay away from the town in the residential part, eastward.

Even in small ways one is continually pulled up by ignorance of the language; it is odd to be unable to carry on a conversation with the servant who answers the front door of a house, yet many of the house servants did not speak English. By the aid of the boy, how-

ever, I arrived at the fact that the Deputy-Commissioner
was at the court house, and, still by the aid of the boy,
I instructed the gharry wallah to drive there.   Even
with the sun-shutters as a protection, the inside of a
gharry at midday is like an oven, and I never felt so
nearly roasted in my life as when I sat outside that
court house waiting to get my note in to the Deputy-
Commissioner, who was engaged in a very important
case.   A hasty line telling me to go to the circuit
house was my reward at length, and, though I felt very
grateful, I did not realise until later the immense boon
which had been bestowed on me, for the Mandalay
circuit house is deservedly famous throughout the land.
It stands in a large compound near the south-eastern
corner of the palace wall overlooking the moat, with a
full view of the Shan hills to the eastward.   It is large
and well built of teak.   On the ground floor is a room
used as a dining-room.   Upstairs are three suites of large
rooms, each with a section of wide verandah cut off from
the next by a partition for a sitting-room, and a bedroom and bath-room behind.   The middle suite I found
occupied on my arrival, so I took the eastern, which was
really far the best, as it commanded a view of the lovely
hills.   The derwan, who was a very respectful and
obliging old man, told me that if I liked he would " do "
for me all day at the reasonable rate of four rupees eight
annas, including afternoon tea, and this I accepted.
The delight of finding myself in these cool, airy, clean
quarters was great.   I sent the boy for the luggage, and,
being very tired and hot with so much rattling about in
the heat of the day, I lay down and had a sweet siesta.

THE MOAT, MANDALAY

BRIDGE OVER THE MOAT, MANDALAY

The four days I passed here were among the happiest I spent in Burma. The severe simplicity of the dark teak surroundings—floor, walls and ceiling—appealed to me, and the views from the open verandah were a constant source of joy.

Right opposite, across the road, was the mirror-like moat, half-covered by flat lotus-leaves, though the lilies themselves were not out at this time. Behind the moat, which was fifty yards in width, rose a high wall of weather-worn red brick with crenelated parapet. Look-out towers or pyathats of a deep maroon colour, with pinnacled, decorated roofs rising storey above storey, adorned the corners and the gates. Mandalay Hill, a conical and not very high hill, rose beyond above the tree tops that were enclosed by the palace wall. To the east were the Shan hills, the edge of the great plateau of elevated land that extends for miles in the centre of the country, and as the sun dropped in the west, lights and colours indescribable appeared in the heights and hollows. They glowed with all the mystery and variety of a jewel, changing every moment.

Along the broad road by the moat came a constant though straggling procession that afforded me never-ending amusement. A purdah woman in brilliant puce, her face hidden in the folds of her garment, a garment so cleverly adjusted that it was robe and skirt and head-dress all in one. Two natives lazily manipulating a little hand-cart, by means of which they drew water from the moat, and sprayed it on the road, arousing such a cloud of steam and dust as showed the roadway to have been well-nigh red-hot. A gharry crammed

K

with well-to-do Burmans, the ends of their pink scarfs fluttering from the windows. A slow-moving bullock-cart, so laden with paddy-straw that the bullocks themselves were half-covered by it. A stout Burman, his lyungi caught halfway up his legs, and his umbrella tucked under his arm, making a brilliant spot of colour in his pink and crimson, as he walked in a businesslike way along the margin of the moat. A rather drabby looking native with a Burman wife, whose strut was even more pronounced than that of the generality of her sisters.

Presently the military band of a native regiment dressed in khaki enlivened the scene. As the afternoon grew late European residents appeared. A motor-car spun past, then a high dog-cart with two ladies in white in it, and so on; the variety of the procession was inexhaustible; it is going on still from day to day, but I no longer can look out on it from the dark teak verandah, except with the eye of memory.

Oh, that verandah, what peaceful days it enshrined for me! The furniture was severely simple but perfectly adequate; a wooden table, a deck chair, an upright chair, a small table, a lamp and a waste-paper basket, and what could any rational being want more? The waste-paper basket was the touch of genius that rounded the whole thing into perfection.

The derwan brought me up a tray with good tea, and toast and jam, which was very welcome. At first one does not mind the toast, which is always exactly the same, with a kind of smoky flavour about it, doubtless from being done at a wood fire; but after a while it palls. I had it twice a day regularly, for the native bread was, to me at least, uneatable. The tea is generally fair, but to get milk is a difficulty. The Burmans do not milk their cows, and think our doing so disgusting. Colonel Yule, in his interesting book *The Mission to the Court of Ava*, suggests that one reason why the cattle in Burma are so flourishing is that the calves get all the milk. Even many of the English residents use condensed milk, finding the real stuff difficult to obtain, and as, of all unpalatable productions, condensed milk is the most abominable, I frequently used a slice of lime instead. English jam is largely imported and easy to get almost everywhere; it was a great boon to me, as the butter varies much and is sometimes uneatable; much of it is tinned, but I discovered that tinned or not it is always improved by washing, a fact that I learned from Chinnasawmy, who used to turn rank yellow stuff into something soft and white like cream cheese.

I did not in the least know how to set about seeing the sights of Mandalay, nor did I even know what they were; I had no guide-book, and Burma is not like England, where one has only to ask. After tea I took a gharry and went to the post-office for my letters; in doing so I had to drive the length of the moat again, and got a clearer idea of it. It is a mile and an eighth long on each of the four sides; on the inner side it is overlooked by the wall which enclosed the old city—not that it was very old, for the whole of Mandalay only dates from 1858. This part is now called the fort, and in the centre lie the congeries of the palace buildings.

The moat is crossed by one bridge in the centre of each side, and an extra one on the west. The four principal bridges lead up to massive entrances in the walls, great gateways painted snowy white, faced by a huge block of masonry for defensive purposes and crowned by a maroon pyathat. The whole effect is very fine. The curiously shaped bridges and the great white artificial cliffs to which they lead up are almost dazzling in the sunshine, casting deep blue shadows; Outside the fort is the new city laid out in rectangles with long straight roads, very broad and very dull. It was very different from my imaginings, which had prompted me to look for dark shadows and wonderful lights, quaint carving and grotesque narrow vistas at every turn. Almost every one expects the same thing of Mandalay and is surprised at the reality. Instead of a city of palaces it is a city of hovels with a palace in the centre. The whole interest and scenic effect linger round the palace and the one or two other objects of interest scattered at some distance from each other.

The post-office is quite near Gales's hotel ; the assistants there were most pleasant and obliging, as indeed I found all the Babus and Eurasians employed in Government service with whom I came in contact. They were particularly so at Mandalay, forwarding my correspondence when I left, and taking a deep personal interest in it. One time when I went there to send off my watch by post, the man in charge asked me what it was, suggested I had done it up inadequately, and invited me inside while he found a suitable box and repacked it himself! The telegraph-office was in

CHINNASAWMY IN DOORWAY OF QUEEN'S
APARTMENTS, MANDALAY

A COURT IN THE PALACE, MANDALAY

another block from the post-office; this is generally so in Burma, the two are kept quite separate. Letters are erratic and undependable, but telegrams can always be relied on, and you may have them any one of three classes, special, ordinary or deferred. Deferred is the most generally used, and the idea is, I suppose, they may be set aside until the line is clear, but they always seemed to go very promptly, and one only pays four annas for ten words, not including address.

I did not do anything else that afternoon, for I was glad enough to get back to that glorious verandah and watch the light glowing in roseate hues on the Shan hills. I heard the occupant of the next suite of rooms striding up and down and talking to a clerk, so was not surprised when eight o'clock came and I descended for dinner, to find him there too. He was an Inspector in the Education Department, and when I explained my position, he very kindly offered to lend me a Burman clerk (than whom there is no better guide), to show me round next day; he said he would not give me his own clerk, but borrow the Deputy Inspector's, and the only man who would "grouse" was the deputy, and that did not matter, with all of which I perfectly agreed. We arranged for the clerk to be there at 7.30 next morning.

Notwithstanding the alarming noises the pigeons or rats made in the high gabled roof, I slept like a top that night. When I awoke I found the whole place bathed in a sheet of white mist. As the sun rose this melted away and every twig and branch dripped refreshingly, while tiny whiffs of steam rose from all over the moat

as if it were hot water.   It was distinctly cooler than it
had been down country.   Punctual to time the Burman
clerk appeared below with a gharry.   He was a nice-
looking, pleasant-mannered boy, dressed native fashion,
with a pink turban ; he salaamed prettily when he saw
me.   I asked him where we should go first and he
suggested the palace and "729" pagodas in the morning, and perhaps the Arakan pagoda, which was rather
far out, in the afternoon.   I wondered where he was
going to sit, for there was no room for him on the box,
and he looked rather too superior to hang on behind the
gharry as Chinna did, but a trifle like that presents no
difficulty to the easy-going Burman.   He scrambled up
past the wild unkempt native driver and jumped on to
the roof, where he enjoyed himself hugely, having a
grand holiday regardless of his superior's "grousing."
His name he told me was Moung Lu Pöe.   We crossed
one of the fascinating maroon and white bridges, rounded
the mass of white masonry defending the gate, and passed
within the walls into a wide open space, with a few
scattered houses and trees and immense tracts of khaki-
coloured grass on which khaki-coloured regiments were
drilling.   It was difficult mentally to reconstruct the
scene as it must have been before the English cleared
out the six thousand houses that stood therein, leaving
the palace free in the centre.   It seemed quite a long
way before we came to the palace, which is not what
we associate with the word at all, but a group or congeries
of detached buildings set at all angles around courts of
various sizes.   They are now open free to all comers,
though formerly the English residents had a club here,

and there was much grumbling when the clubites were forced to go elsewhere.

The buildings are all of one storey; even the great seven-roofed spire of the King's House, the most imposing of all, is a sham, having no upper stories. This peculiarity is due to the fact of the Burman's great dislike to knowing that another man's feet are over his head.

There is a certain similarity between the buildings, and the general impression is that of wonderful vistas and gorgeous detail, with the blackest shadows and glowing light. In one of the courts there was a large bougainvillea, whose royal magenta blossoms showed up startlingly against the white walls near. Dark interiors were unexpectedly lit up by gleams falling upon the stout red and gold columns, and some of the apartments were completely panelled with mirror-mosaic of fine design : as its garishness was toned by age the effect was good. Through the dark gloom of the unwindowed rooms, through bright courts and again into gloom, the eye was carried on from door to door to see at last perhaps the figure of a guardian in a dark blue uniform and red sash standing motionless framed in light. The gleam of a dark green balustrade caught the attention, and though it was made of nothing but a row of glass bottles the detail is not unhandsome. In the Queen's apartments the mirrors on the walls are hand-painted with flowers, and the walls of another room near are entirely carved and perforated. The golden seven-roofed spire springs gracefully through the soda-water bottle shape to a golden htee. Beneath this is the huge gilt throne set thick with looking-glass panels, and founded on living human flesh and blood :—

"Mandalay was commenced in 1858. . . . When the foundations of the city wall were laid fifty-two persons of both sexes, and of various age and rank, were consigned to a living tomb. Three were buried under each of the twelve city gates, one at each of the four corners, one under each of the palace gates, and at the corners of the timber stockade, and four beneath the throne itself. The selection had to be made with care, for the victims were required to be representative people, born on special days of the week, and the boys buried were not to have any tattoo marks on them, the girls not to have their ears bored. When it was known that the troops were making the collection, no one was to be seen about the streets except in great bands in the middle of the day. The Government gave a series of magnificent dramatic entertainments, but no one went to see them. Eventually, however, the tale was made up and the building went on apace." *

The steps of the golden throne were oftentimes crowded with princes of the blood-royal, all of whom were destined to come to a violent death by the fears of the reigning monarch. The doors of the throne-room are elaborately carved and gilt. I took a photo of my guide sitting in one of them, but unfortunately the scaffolding belonging to some repairs then going on has spoiled the effect. In the Hall of Audience near the throne-room are rows of stately gold pillars which, when

* "The Burman: His Life and Notions." By Sir J. G. Scott, K.C.I.E.

MOUNG LU PÖE AT THE DOOR OF THE
THRONE-ROOM, MANDALAY

47

THE KING'S HOUSE, MANDALAY

the sun gets low and strikes in horizontally, glow as if they were transparent. The only other two points of interest in the grounds are the high wooden watch-tower, which is worth ascending because of the view, and the museum, where may be seen quaint little figures dressed in the costumes of the old court, a style of dress still always adopted at the Pwés or plays. The palace was built during the reign of King Mindon, the predecessor of Theebaw, and the capital was then transferred here. The Burmese were very fond of changing their capitals, and numbers of old cities can claim to have been chief of the country in their time.

The English had annexed Tennasserim, Arakan and part of Martaban in 1826, and the Pegu district after the second war in 1852. The Burmese king at this time refused to cede any part of the country which had been conquered by the British, and it was useless to attempt to get him to sign any treaty defining the boundary between what remained to him of the country and that taken by the English. Therefore the Viceroy, Lord Dalhousie, drew a line across the map following a parallel of latitude and declared that to be the boundary, a sensible proceeding, but one which would probably nowadays call forth a howl from the Little Englanders.

King Mindon died in 1878 and was succeeded by one of his thirty sons, namely Theebaw, whose mother had made herself mistress of the palace. Theebaw's reign of bloodshed and cruelty went from bad to worse. Only a short time after his accession he ordered a massacre of the majority of his relatives. All who did not escape

8

were seized and either beaten to death with bludgeons or half strangled. The bodies of the women and children, in some cases only half dead, were pitched into a large pit prepared for them and the earth stamped down ; it is said that it moved uneasily for three days subsequently. The corpses of the men, the royal princes, were thrown into the Irrawaddy, having been conveyed there in eight cart-loads. The whole holocaust included about eighty victims. The remonstrances of the British Resident were treated with contempt ; massacres and cruelties continued remorselessly. In 1884 they reached their height, when the number of men, women and children brutally murdered in a short time was between two and three hundred.

"On the day after the chief massacre the corpses were carted out of the city, and were exposed for some days in the burial-ground on the west. Here they remained mutilated, putrefying, and uncovered with earth to show how terrible a thing it was to incur the royal displeasure. Hands and legs were hacked off to loosen the prison irons, before the putrefying bodies were thrown, in heaps of four and five together, into shallow graves, and given an insufficient covering of about a foot of earth. While these atrocities were being perpetrated —and pigs and pariah dogs unearthed the corpses and battened on the loathsome feast thus plentifully provided for them by the inhumanity of the king, his consort, and his ministers—high festival was being held within the palace. Theatrical performances were given continuously night after night." *

* "Burma under British Rule and Before." By John Nisbet.

" Fresh massacres took place in the capital; bands of robbers infested the country and raided at will into the British territory; the greater part of the tributary Shan States rose in rebellion and the whole of Upper Burma became disorganised, with the inevitable result of a paralysis of our trade." *

At length in October 1885 the British Government took notice of the cries and bloodshed, and sent a force to advance on Mandalay, an expedition which ended in the annexation of Upper Burma, when Theebaw was exiled, to spend the remainder of his life in durance in India.

This book is nothing but a personal travel-book and does not profess to treat in any way of the history of Burma, but it is impossible to avoid thus touching very slightly on the scenes of horror so recently enacted in the great open spaces now lying peacefully beneath the cloudless sky. Bloodshed and cruelty seemed far enough off on that glorious morning when I wandered through the sunlit courts ablaze with sunshine, and was watched curiously by the quiet guardians.

We left the palace by the eastern gate and went straight to the famous shrines of Kutho-daw or the Royal Merit House built by Theebaw's uncle, where the whole of the Buddhist scriptures are inscribed on black slabs enclosed in small shrines. This is known by various names, among which the most popular is the 729 pagodas. The shrines are all arranged in parallel lines on the sides of a square, in the midst of which rises a white pagoda. They are not very large, and each one has a

* Sir J. G. Scott, K.C.I.E.

little dome at the top, and is pierced by four openings showing within the slab of black stone like a tombstone, beautifully inscribed with the scriptures. By mounting to the platform of the central pagoda a very good idea can be gained of the whole. The whiteness of the little white shrines is emphasised here and there by rich and heavy evergreen shrubs, and behind may be seen the far-away hills.

Not very far from the Kutho-daw are some interesting choungs, and also the Incomparable Pagoda, which was partly burnt not long ago. This is surrounded by a row of small shrines, in each of which is a roughly made figure of a poongyi kneeling in adoration. Behind rises Mandalay Hill, of no very great height, though it entails a rough scramble to get to the summit. It is covered with scrub, and is a fine place in which to encounter snakes. From the top there is a wide view of the great plain in which Mandalay lies, and from one point a very striking glimpse of the Kutho-daw. After this expedition I returned to lunch and rest, asking Moung Lu Pöe to come again at 4.30 to take me out, to which he willingly agreed. I found the derwan had provided a very good breakfast of several courses, including, of course, curry, and that my friend the Education Inspector had departed.

At 4.30 punctually my guide arrived with a gharry and we started off for the Arakan pagoda of which I had heard so much. This is a long drive, two or three miles at least, and anything but pleasant. The way seemed to go on endlessly over very dusty wide roads, with medium-sized trees beside them, also white with dust.

48

S. H. Reynolds

THE KUTHO-DAW, MANDALAY

49

S. H. Reynolds

A STREET SCENE, MANDALAY

It seems impossible that people can live healthily in such a welter of dust ; they must breathe it and eat it continually. The roads were lined mostly by small huts, many of them dilapidated, with the framework very much askew, and the plaited mats which formed the walls frayed at the edges. They were well spaced out, standing apart from one another with dusty growth of tree or plantain beside them. All the huts were raised two or three feet from the ground, and beneath them swarmed huge goats and enormous black pigs like boars, skinny hens, and naked children. The houses were often quite open in front, and domestic arrangements went on in full view of all the neighbours. It was curious to see the handwork done outside in the roadway, and how the trades tended to segregate. One man was working at good wicker chairs, and a row of chair-makers would be near him ; then came a colony of shoemakers, the red and emerald velvet toes showing up gaily. The manufacture of little wooden toys painted in gaudy colours is a favourite industry in the neighbourhood of the pagoda. A row of sewing-machines would proclaim a colony of dhurzies, and then in the middle of all the dirt, right in the roadway, I saw a man cooking flat cakes on a kind of gridiron.

At length we saw the Arakan pagoda, but it is hemmed in, and does not stand to such advantage as the Shwe Dagôn. Outside the entrance were two immense leogryphs, passing between which we went up a long arcade, but to my great disappointment the stalls were nearly all shut and the place deserted, Moung Lu Pöe told me the people went away early on account of the plague. I asked him if he were afraid of infection, but he shook his head with a smile.

The great feature of the pagoda is the huge golden Buddha of peculiar sanctity. This was brought from Arakan in 1784, and to it the pagoda owes its name. When we came round to the shrine where it was I found a crowd of some twenty or thirty people bowing and intoning their monotonous chant. Rows of small candles, stuck by their grease on to the floor, were guttering in the draught before the great image. Moung Lu Pöe told me I might pass in front of the crowd without offence, and holding my muslin skirts so as not to catch alight, I did so. The Buddha is colossal, but so hemmed in by his straitened walls that he is not seen to advantage. One or two Burmans were arranging a kind of paper robe around him, which my guide explained was to "take care of him," for though his face is brass, and not gold, like Mah Shwe Bwin's Buddha, his body is all covered with gold leaf. The expression of his brazen countenance is hard and cruel, and he wears a great tiara like a pope. The Woondouk, a Burmese official, said to Major Phayre, of the 1855 embassy: "It is a faithful representation of the living original. When the Lord Gaudama visited Arakan, Chanda Surya was the king of that country. The Buddha being about to depart, the king prayed him to leave his blessed resemblance and substitute with them as some consolation for his absence. The Buddha consented. Several attempts were made to cast an image, but they all failed. At length, by the divine interposition, the present image was successfully obtained." (Col. Yule.)

This accounts for the great veneration with which the image is regarded. When it is considered that it is about twelve feet high and of solid brass, to bring it over the Arakan Yoma seems a remarkable feat. It is supposed to have been brought in several pieces.

It was a strange sensation to be standing in that small chamber surrounded closely by those people separated by such gulfs of tradition and racial characteristics from me. In the semi-dimness the voices chanted louder and louder for my benefit, and the men aloft grinned down and asked my Burman if I would like the cloth or robe removed. I assented at once, and they disclosed the gold leaf with which the brazen body of the image is lavishly encrusted by the devotion of generations. As I passed out three haggard old nuns set upon me with cries for pice. I happened to have three, though such small coins rarely came my way, so I gave them into one skinny clutching hand, meaning its owner to share them with the others; not a bit of it, having got them she incontinently bolted, and the others clamoured more wildly than before. I had no more pice, but produced a two anna bit. Moung Lu Pöe promptly intercepted it as I was about to give it to them, and explaining that it was far too much for a donation, took it to a stall to get it changed. He failed in his quest, and then asked one of the toothless old crones for change. From some mysterious fold in her drab garments she produced a dirty bit of rag in which were knotted seven pice. My wise guide thereupon gave each of the old women one pice on condition that they went away, which they did.

I bought some of the cheap and gaudy tigers and monkeys sold here, which delight children, and after strolling round the pagoda we returned to the gharry. My guide told me he was now going to show me the Queen's choung, otherwise called the Golden Monastery, and away we jolted merrily, he still enjoying his exalted position on the roof.   The Queen's choung is one of those things which no one who visits Mandalay should fail to see.   It is a perfectly magnificent building, standing in a very large parawoon or compound over-shadowed by large trees.   Loathsome pariah dogs of very large size rushed out to bark at us, making the air resound with their yelps.   The neighbourhood of a choung attracts many of their kind, for the overflowing begging-bowls of the poongyis provide an ample surplus for such undesirable pensioners.   Though the noise the dogs make is terrifying to any one nervous, they are not ferocious ; never having been unkindly treated, they have no cause to hate man.   By nature curs, they slink away at the merest threat of a stick or stone, and it is well it is so, for a bite from mouths such as theirs would probably be poisonous.

A mighty trunk lay prostrate in the compound, and the yellow-robed brethren swarmed around it, rolling it along over the smooth ground.   This sight surprised me, as I was under the impression they did no physical work at all, but this my guide contradicted ; he said the log had evidently been a present to them, and they were going to cut it up for their own use.   They all stopped their work to stare at us, but taking no heed of them, we went on toward the choung.

S. H. Reynolds

THREE HAGGARD OLD NUNS

51

S. H. Reynolds

THE GOLDEN MONASTERY, MANDALAY

It rose in a seven-fold roof in tiers of rusty gold high against the thrilling blue of the sky. Every square inch of the walls was carved and covered with gilt; when the sun caught one corner it shone out radiating rich light. The choungs I saw were all on the same pattern; the ground floor is unused and is, in fact, merely an open space between posts which serves as a playground for the boys who are taught in the choung. A short flight of steps leads to a verandah, from the centre of which rises the main building; in this as in other Burman buildings there is but one storey, though the impression is of many. I peeped into a sort of broad corridor which ran round it opening on to the verandah, and saw several poongyis lying about in sleepy content on mats and mattresses. Some children had followed us up out of curiosity, and among them was one small boy with the shaven poll and yellow raiment of the neophyte; he looked so very young that I asked his age and was told he was only ten. By this time several of the poongyis themselves had joined us, and stood close around with their curious yellowish faces repeating the hue of their garments; their beetle-brown eyes were unpleasant, and their expression sensual and lowering. The life they lead, in its perpetual sloth and lack of interest, is not one to encourage spirituality, and it is wonderful that worse results do not arise from it. These particular poongyis had evidently no scruple about looking at a woman, or perhaps a white woman did not count in their code; anyway they came very near indeed, and scrutinised me so eagerly that I should not have been surprised to feel their long thin parch-

T

ment fingers in contact with my dress.   Though they
refrained from actually touching me, they asked many
questions of my guide, and when at last I inquired if I
might see inside the shrine they assented gleefully, as
proud as children to show off their treasures.

The first moment I entered the gloom of the hall
after the brilliancy of the sunshine outside, I could see
nothing but outlines of pillars; then, as my pupils
enlarged, I made out various objects heavily carved.
The poongyis lit a candle and gave it to Moung Lu Pöe
to hold, then they almost tumbled over each other in
their extremé eagerness to point out the rich design of
the wood carving that ran along the balustrade surrounding the shrine.   It was in extraordinarily high
relief, undercut to the depth of two or three inches, and
represented babies and dragons, fruit and flowers.   I was
then invited further up into the holy of holies.   Once
again for a moment there came over me almost over-
poweringly that sense of strange aloneness; here in the
dimness with only one flickering candle was I surrounded by a people so utterly alien in habit, religion
and thought that the gulf seemed verily impassable, but
the moment passed and I looked on them once more as
I had done, as children.

Then a cloth was removed, and the greatest treasure
of all was exhibited; it was Gautama's tooth, a tusk
about the size of my little finger, resembling a boar's
tusk, poised on wire over a bunch of wax flowers in a
glass case.   Moung Lu Pöe was anxious to impress on
me the very great honour it was for me to see it, as
such a holy relic is usually buried in the heart of a

mighty pagoda, and in any case is rarely shown to a stranger, and I did my best to live up to the expectations of my appreciation.

The poongyis asked through the interpreter where I came from, and when I told them London they repeated it in various odd intonations. I tried to carry on some conversation, inquiring how they spent their days; they replied they prayed and taught, but when I expressed a wish to see the schoolboys I was told, "boys dismissed."

As I finally moved away I asked my guide if I should give them anything, but he said they were forbidden to take money, so I could only wish them a cordial good-bye, and left them standing there rather blankly, as if the unwonted excitement had left a flatness behind.

This was on a Friday. I spent the whole of the next day in Mandalay too. The bazaar is well worth visiting; it is all very modern and clean and neat, utterly different from the dark noisy narrow alleys of the Moulmein bazaar. Here one can see in perfection the dainty little Burmese maidens, who run about and laugh, and even put their arms round you if you give them the least encouragement. At one stall in particular, C 12, I was fascinated by the glory of the silks; especially by the peculiar yellow that one can get nowhere else, which turns to saffron and orange and gold, all in different folds. Here were also lovely mauves and blues, though these are not fashionable Burmese colours. When we passed on to a second stall, the keeper of the first, a dainty little maiden, ran after us, and, through

the boy, said she could show us another good stall
where were many other kinds of silk. We followed her
and she led us promptly back to her own, a specimen
of ingenious trading not without its humour.

I had meant to leave at eight o'clock on Sunday
morning on the Irrawaddy Flotilla Company's cargo-
boat going up to Bhamo, because I had been told she
carried a bazaar aboard, and that the Burmans came
down from all the river-side villages to buy, affording a
series of pictures well worth seeing. But, alas ! I heard
from the agent that the cargo-boat had not come down,
no one knew where she was, probably stuck on a sandbank ; the one fact certain was that she could not
possibly start north again on Sunday morning. This
was a disappointment, as, if I went by train to Katha, and
then by river to Bhamo, I missed much good scenery,
and especially the great bell at Mengohn. However,
there was no help for it, so I made preparations to leave
Mandalay by the midday train on Monday, and reluctantly parted from the city where I had spent four
really happy days.

52

S.H. Reynolds

A POONGYI

S. H. Reynolds

BALUSTRADE AT THE GOLDEN MONASTERY,
MANDALAY

CHAPTER VIII

TO THE FAR NORTH

MANDALAY is generally the limit for the flying tourist who rushes up from Rangoon by train and goes down by mail-boat, giving barely one day to the famous royal city, but a certain number of tourists penetrate as far as Bhamo, which is perhaps half as far north of Mandalay as Mandalay is from Rangoon. Though the distance is shorter the journey is longer, and the route by rail involves some complication. One leaves Mandalay at mid-day and arrives at daybreak at a junction called Naba; here a change is made to a little branch line which deposits one on the river's bank at Katha—the remainder of the main line running on to Myitkhyina. The steamer which leaves Katha daily in the middle of the morning goes slowly through the grand scenery of the Middle Defile and ties up for the night above it, moving on again the following day, so as to get to Bhamo about eleven.

Besides my disappointment at missing so much of the river by taking rail to Katha, there was the crawl down to Amarapura again, and the ferry at Sagaing to negotiate, and the disagreeable necessity of spending a night on the none too clean cushions of the railway carriage, but it had to be faced. The station-master at Mandalay was extremely civil and obliging, and I had a carriage to myself, so I could not grumble. After crossing the river and climbing the sandbank to Sagaing station I was rewarded by an unexpected and pretty sight. The platform was crowded with fruit-sellers squatting beside baskets in which their golden and ruddy wares were piled high, glowing in the rich sunlight.

Burmese stations are an inexhaustible source of interest, but they are rarely so attractive as Sagaing was that afternoon, with oranges gleaming between the wide meshes of the cunningly contrived baskets, and great piles of green water-melons and rose-apples. At every station there is a sweeper, in a turban and loin-cloth, which have presumably once been white. He has a large switch broom and assiduously brushes up the dust into every one's face ; the intention is laudable but the practice disagreeable. The people travel extensively ; there is constantly a crowd on the platform, and how they chatter, a rookery is nothing to it, a "rookery" of magpies would be the only equivalent anywhere near. At one place some one spilt a basket of green tomatoes down beside the train on the line, and the yelling and rushing and gabbling were such that I thought some one had at least cut a hand off inadvertently. The food-sellers too made themselves heard abundantly; they went up and down carrying large pannier baskets swung on a bamboo, like a gigantic pair of scales. These were filled with a sickening mixture that made one's stomach turn even to look at it. Bad fish, yellow cakes, cigars, a kind of dried mush, and whole peas welded into rings and circles.

The trains do their best to act in keeping with their stations, it would not do to have a straightforward dull kind of train in such a scene as that. Sometimes they start out quite hopefully after waiting only a comparatively short time at any platform, then before they are well clear of it stop again and settle down ; at last they take courage and dawdle along to the next station, perhaps about five miles off, here they apparently take root. At length the guard waves first the green flag and then the red one and then both together, but finding the engine-driver takes no notice, he pretends he was only flicking the flies away and resumes his conversation with the station-master. Suddenly, when he has forgotten all about it, the train goes off, scattering all the pariah dogs, and hens, and goats, and people who have been strolling about among the wheels. There is a running and jump-ing on to the foot-boards, and for the next three or four minutes many a dark face passes your window as its owner works himself back to his own compartment along the foot-board. When fairly under way, however, the trains go a good pace and get over the ground well ; these are only minor incidents. When we had left Sagaing we stopped a long time a little further on, and though it was still the height of the afternoon, the sky became overcast and a cold wind seemed to be blowing about mysteriously. I noticed it, and thought how strange a thing it was to happen in this cloudless country, but presently the sun shone again and I forgot to speculate on the gloom and unexpected darkness. Not until a fortnight later did I learn that I had missed an eclipse of the sun, when I might have seen it by putting my head out of the carriage window! Such is fate!

We ran on through rather uninteresting country but as the sun sank I saw a fine panorama unroll before me.

The line is single, there are no embankments, the windows run right along the sides of the carriages, so whatever view there is is seen uninterruptedly and in great comfort. We passed along by the edge of a vast mere or marsh just as the sun, three times his apparent size, was setting. The water turned almost blood-red, and was broken by clumps of bushes and tall reeds, and peopled by long stringing flights of wild-fowl. When the sun set, that indescribable warm golden glow so full of "tone" succeeded, and then darkness dropped as sharply as when a candle is blown out. On little low-lying spits of land camp-fires sprang up, and I got a glimpse of natives fishing : over all was the queer sort of smell of burnt wood which I shall ever associate with Burma. It seemed to me I was in a dream, for the air was neither hot nor cold, just the atmosphere of a dream, and the vastness of the empty plain was eerie, when suddenly from out the darkness standing on a piece of waste land, utterly alone, there seemed to spring a great image of Buddha, pure white, and three or four times life-size. It was sheltered by a rough thatch roof, supported on poles, and in front was a long row of little cheap candles burning brightly and straight in the still air.

At Schwebo we stopped for dinner, and I made the

FRUIT-SELLERS AT SAGAING

MERRY CHILDHOOD

acquaintance of the only other European in the train, an elderly man, an engineer, going up to Bhamo, and beyond over the hills into China, to report on a railway which might possibly come into being.

Afterwards I slept comfortably in the train as we hurried on through the night. When I awoke in the morning the air was as thick with mist as it often is on a November day in England and everything was dripping with moisture. However, here you have one certainty, that it is not going to continue so all day, the sun's fiery rays will soon send the mist flying. Near Naba, where we had to change at about seven o'clock, I got my first glimpse of real jungle, great feathery clumps of bamboo with little tracks leading between, and huge broad-leaved plants, and thick creepers. At Naba it was possible to get some tea, and we soon started on the little branch line that slowly climbed up an immense height and then dropped down again to the river at Katha. The rail between Naba and Katha ran through one of the prettiest parts I had yet seen, and I saw it well, as there was a kind of cab or platform at the rear end of the carriage, on which I could stand to watch the scenery, as we crawled upward at a foot's pace. There was real jungle on each side, great teak trees, impenetrable bushes and creepers, and innumerable mighty bamboos. Many of the smaller plants had bright red leaves and all were glistening in the morning moisture. Behind, high hills rose to perhaps a thousand feet, clothed with forest to the very top. To me the charm was intensified by the freshness of everything; it was so unsullied, so untrodden. When one views a

U

similar bit of scenery at, say, the Scottish lakes, one
knows that people pour over it in their hundreds every
day in the season, and the bloom is gone.

It was quite hot when we arrived at the station where
we were to board the steamer, and she was waiting for
us.   Oddly enough, she goes by the name of the ferry-
boat, though the whole day and part of the next one is
occupied by her trip up-stream ; they have odd ideas of
ferry-boats in this part.   If I had been able to come by
cargo-boat, as intended, all the way from Mandalay I
should have come right past here without changing.
The ferry-boat was quite comfortable, with a small
saloon deck forward, roofed-in and protected by awnings,
and here I and the engineer spent a peaceful day together.
The wide placid river, the blue hills, the endless sandbanks filed past monotonously until we reached a place
called Schwegu, which at once stood out apart from
others.   It is on a cliff-like height crowned by palms,
pagodas and choungs.   A long flight of wooden steps
leads up to the heights, on the edge of which were
seated, like large parroquets, the most gaudily dressed
people I had yet seen.   They rather reminded me of
Swiss peasants in their costumes, for they were wearing
short red skirts and leggings, blue bodices with red
sleeves, and had a broad red band across the breast.
They belonged to the tribe of Palaungs.   On their
heads was a kind of hood edged with white, which fell
back so as to form a long cloak behind.

It was at Schwegu also that I saw some Afghans on
the beach, big bearded men, who stood out markedly
amid the little beardless Burmans.

After this we drew near to the entrance of the Middle Defile ; the banks of the river were lined by a rich lush growth that glowed green-gold as the sun struck it at an acute angle, then the hills grew higher and closed in on each side, and a damp woody smell crept out across the water.   Sir J. G. Scott describes the lowest defile (the one I failed to see, not being able to come all the way up-stream) as being formed simply by " high banks covered with dense vegetation," and puts, pithily, the difference between the three defiles thus : " The first defile may be called pleasing, the second striking, the third savage "; so I certainly had the best of it in seeing the two I did.

Huge trees with white stems as straight as telegraph posts stood out against the dense foliage, and wreaths, and ropes and shawls of creeper flung themselves from one to the other.   There was a wide clearing as sharp as a knife-edge down the side of one hill, and for a considerable time this puzzled us greatly until my companion rightly surmised it was the clearing for a new telegraph wire.

As the hills grew steeper it looked as if we must run up against a dead end ; but we turned a corner almost at right angles, and saw a towering cliff which dropped sheer down to the water.   It is one of the grandest sights in the defiles, and as we saw it, black against the evening sky, we lost nothing in the setting.   About a third of the way up on a mighty rock stands a pagoda, looking like a child's toy, though, I am told, it is sixty feet high

The current did not seem swift, it was so very smooth,

and we went slowly with the oily swell falling away almost without a sound ; there were no birds, only the unearthly silence of falling night.   As the shadows grew darker a weird hoot sounded out suddenly ; it was our syren to warn rafts ahead that we were coming, for to meet one of the hundred-foot rafts in such a place as this at a narrow bend would mean disaster.   Just as we turned a sharp corner two flaring dropping torches shone out, and drawing nearer to them slowly we saw two naked figures, like the bronze statues modelled to hold lamps, standing with outstretched arms at each end of an enormous raft.   Then we were through the defile and moored for the night, for the river channel is too dangerous to traverse in the dark.   The whole of the forepart of the deck was awninged in and made a cosy room.   It was absolutely still except for the ceaseless chattering of the native crew as they foregathered round a wood fire on the beach.

CHAPTER IX

THE WAY TO CHINA

WE were not long in getting to Bhamo the next morning, and so smoothly did the steamer start that I never knew she was moving until I came out of my cabin. We agreed to have breakfast earlier than usual, and before we had finished we came in sight of the town rising from the low sandy shore. My companion pointed out to me the lower landing-place or ghaut where the steamers are compelled to stop when the river is lowest, but as it was in fairly good current now we came within a mile of the town, from which we were separated by an appalling waste of soft sand like a miniature desert. There were several flats or great barges moored near, and as crowds of curious faces, more or less Mongolian in type, peered out of them I realised I had got into the land of the Chino-Burmans.

We had hardly stopped before a clerk from the Deputy-Commissioner's office came up to me on board and said he had been sent by the Deputy-Commissioner, who was himself away, to look after me and tell me al I wanted to know. He had procured a stout wooden cane-seated chair, slung on two bamboos, to convey me across the wilderness of sand. This was carried by two sturdy men of the Shan tribe. It was my first sight of the Shans, the great race which ranks only second to the Burmans themselves in the occupation of the country. They were not very tall, but as strong as bullocks, with hugely developed swelling muscles standing out on their red leathery shoulders and arms. They were dressed in loose blue blouses, very wide short trousers, and folded turbans of what looked like dark blue serge. To tell the truth I envied them their job even less than I appreciated my own share in the performance, for I am no feather-weight. The sensation of being hoisted up shoulder-high had to be endured with some fortitude, and when they set off at a jog-trot, out of step, and stumbling in the soft sand, I lost sight of all dignity and only clutched at equilibrium. Mr. E., the clerk, having seen that the boy had got a bullock-cart for the things, followed. And when we finally reached firm ground he was there, panting, beside me. The ride was costly, for I had to give the men a rupee; but all experience, especially that of a painful kind, is apt to be so. Mr. E. and I then entered a gharry, and he told me that I should have to go to the dâk bungalow, as the railway party, of which my friend the engineer was the chief, had arrived before him and were already occupying the circuit house. As it turned out, this arrangement was what I should have chosen, for the verandah of the dâk bungalow commands a view in its way as interesting as that of the Mandalay circuit house.

Bhamo was the Mecca of my pilgrimage. Only a short distance off over the blue hills lies the Chinese border, and the weird races that pour in from the northern

hills are much more individual and characteristic than
those one sees in the south. The few tourists who do
extend their trip in the country as far as Bhamo nearly
all come up by steamer and return again the next day
on the same boat, whereby they miss a great deal. It
is true that Bhamo is a dead-end for those who have not
private facilities, for the Flotilla Company's steamers do
not go above it; but I should imagine that one could
pleasantly fill a week in Bhamo itself. Anyway, I was
to be one of the lucky ones, for a letter from headquarters had requested the Deputy-Commissioner at
Bhamo to leave the Government launch at my disposal
when I required it, and I had wired a few days before
to tell him the date of my coming. He was away at
Myitkhyina, far northward, from whence he would return
in a borrowed launch, having left the little *Indaw* for me
as requested. Yet I could not start away the next day,
as for two days a month the Upper Defile is closed to
allow of the passage of the trunks and logs belonging to
the forest firm of Steel Brothers, and no traffic can go up.
As it happened, the day of my arrival and the morrow
were these days. However, that did not matter, for I
imagined I should find ample entertainment in Bhamo
itself on Thursday, to say nothing of the necessity of
getting some stores, as I understood there was practically
nothing at all on the launch.

The dâk bungalow looked rather dark and mosquitoey
when we arrived at it, as it stands in the shade of a
clump of heavily foliaged mango-trees, but this impression soon faded in view of the intense interest of the
prospect from the verandah. Mr. E. left me, promising

to come again and take me to see anything I wanted.

The bungalow is small, standing on legs, with an exterior staircase leading straight on to the verandah, which is also the common dining-room. Luckily when I arrived I had the whole place to myself. Later I managed to get a photo of this verandah by means of a long exposure, but the result hardly gives an impression of the delightful bareness of the place. The uncovered floor-boards do not show, my cushion lying on a chair is transformed into a detail of elegance, and the table-cloth, which was none of the whitest and very coarse, might be of damask. On to this verandah two bed-rooms, each with its small bath-room behind, open. Looking out from the verandah I could see a wide stretch of bare burnt-up ground, broken by a few small trees and shrubs, and ending in a range of high hills of a marvellous milk-blue, as different as could be from the rich, clear dark blue of Scottish hills after rain. This wide space was crossed by a raised causeway, and as I sat, lost in dreams, many times in the few following days, I heard the tinkle of distant mule-bells, and then a slow heavily laden caravan would steal across the road, kicking up clouds of dust, amid which trotted the drivers in huge cartwheel hats and wide white Chinese trousers. It was "the road to China," and China lay only some thirty to forty miles away there in the hills. Or there broke in upon my silence the slower, more sonorous sound of an elephant bell, and a mighty elephant with his mahout on his neck would stride across my picture. My deck chair was the throne from which a series of real

THE PAGODA IN THE MIDDLE DEFILE,
IRRAWADDY

VERANDAH OF THE DÂK BUNGALOW,
BHAMO

"living pictures" were continually to be seen. I was near other races, other countries, which had hitherto only been names to me. The smaller details in the immediate foreground also reminded me I was far from England—the unripe mangoes hanging on the trees, the squawking of the crows, and the occasional startling shriek of another bird resembling a jay. Neither he nor the crows minded the mere clapping of hands; it took a bodily rush to make them change their quarters. At first I could not understand the use of a wide-meshed wire netting that one could pull down over the openings of the verandah, but experience soon taught me, for when I left a tin of chocolates on the table one day the lid was off on my return, and the chocolates, which were wrapped separately in silver paper, were scattered in every direction.

The derwan looked an old villain, but was really civil enough. As he could not speak a word of English, I had to await the arrival of Chinnasawmy with the luggage before I could communicate my lordly wishes to him. I found his charges were the usual ones, viz., eight annas for chota hazri, one rupee eight annas for breakfast, eight annas for tea, and two rupees for dinner, with an additional charge of four annas daily for the sweeper. The tea and toast and jam were all a little inferior to those at Mandalay, but did well enough. When I had finished, the Deputy Commissioner's wife sent her buggy round to take me for a drive, so that I gained some idea of the place, which is quite peculiar and not at all easy to grasp at first. It is intersected in all directions by curious raised roads, necessary because in

x

the wet season the intermediate parts become lakes. In some of the hollows, dry at this season, were well-kept market gardens attended by Chinamen. There is a fort where the military live, two good polo grounds, and a circular drive cut through the jungle, round which we went. At one place we came to a finger-post, on one fork of which was written in English, "The way to China," and my heart gave a great throb to think I was so near to a country which had always seemed to me as unattainable as the moon! There is a little English outpost in the hills called Sinlôn, only to be reached on horseback—would that time had allowed me to go there!

The place is unique, and there is much to see. One of the most striking objects is a pure white bell-pagoda, which stands out against the blue hills from many points of view. The colour of the hills as I saw them that after-noon was indeed beyond anything I could have imagined, and it was pure, not emphasised by any complement. There it was rising sheer from the low ground, one glorious sheet of blue that stirred one's heart like a glad song. In the midst of the town, for town it must be called, though it is not in the least like one, are a number of worn and crumbling grey pagodas, and near them the long neat wooden court-house, with three or four khaki-clad policemen outside as symbols of law and order. All kinds of religions are represented ; there is a bright new Mohammedan mosque and a very celebrated joss-house ; also a sort of open temple where the ceremony of initiation into the Buddhist monastic order takes place.

By the time I returned from the drive the sun had fallen, and the air felt very cold indeed. I was glad to draw down the mat blinds provided on the verandah, and should not at all have minded a fire, but there was no provision for one. At any rate I was free from mosquitoes ; I had been bothered slightly by the attentions of one or two at Mandalay, though I had been told I should meet with none "up-country" in the cold weather. However, it was not advisable to do without mosquito curtains, for there were other things about, as I found on going into my bedroom soon after eleven. For on the bare whitewashed walls was an immense spider, whose outstretched legs, wider in circuit than the palm of my hand, were striped with yellow. Chinnasawmy and the derwan had long ago retired to the go-down near the compound gate or to make festival in the town with friendly spirits, so if the beast were to be killed I must do the slaying myself, and that I very much objected to for several reasons. I knew he was a tarantula, about whose bite I had heard deadly things, and I could never have slept in peace until the deed was done. It took me some time and the heel of a slipper to accomplish it, for he ran so fast, but I succeeded at last and threw his crumpled body out of the window. Only once again did I meet with one of his kind, and that was when I was dressing for dinner one night in Rangoon and a similar monster ran across my dressing-table. The boy slew him with a rolled-up newspaper, and we carried him downstairs to hear him pronounced to be undoubtedly a tarantula.

In the early hours of the morning I awoke trembling

with cold, and getting up, gradually dragged everything I had on the top of me before I could get warm. The whole world was wreathed in mist, and even at eight o'clock the ground was still white with frost, real hoar-frost clinging to every blade and twig.

I think it was this morning that poor Chinnasawmy came to me and said he was cold. I reminded him he had bought a long coat, and he answered, " Coat only come to here, Missie," marking off a place about his knees. " Legs is cold ! "

I looked hopelessly at the thin white garment he wore swathed around his legs, and asked, " But what can you wear ? "

" Trouseys, Missie," he said hopefully.

" I'm not going to buy you trousers," said I, " so you need not think it."

" Drawerses, Missie."

" Well," I said doubtfully, " you may buy a pair of woven drawers if you like ; I'll give you three rupees, and anything over you must pay yourself."

He could not get them, however, in Bhamo, so had to wait till he returned to Mandalay, where he bought them at a kind of general store, half Europeanised, where one could get most things or substitutes for them, and he proudly laid them on the seat of the gharry for me to see, with the bill for three rupees eight annas.

It is not necessary in Bhamo to be out too early, for the sun is not unbearable all day at this time of the year ; thus it was comparatively late when Mr. E. called for me and we went for a walk round the town. We visited the market-place first, and here I saw such

KACHIN WOMAN AND GIRL

ON THE HEIGHTS BY THE RIVER, SCHWEGU

a bewildering crowd of strange peoples and strange costumes that the impression is still all blurred. Mongolian faces met one at every turn; it seemed to me that Chinese blood was far more in evidence than Burmese.

The most notable and striking people were the Shans, fair and ruddy of face, small and sturdy of stature; men and women alike were wearing the dark blue tunic and short skirts or very full trousers, which make such a convenient working dress. Some had blue turbans and some enormous cart-wheel pith hats.

They struck me as having more backbone and more go in them than the Burmans, but they have not their essential aristocracy; they look what they are, hewers of wood and drawers of water. Their cheery, good-tempered faces showed that their lives agreed with them. Behind, at a little distance, the men reminded me most oddly of the Highlanders of Scotland, the blue trousers are so short and full that they fall like a kilt, the bare knees are shown above the leggings which take the place of stockings, the blue cloth turban does duty for a Glengarry even to the little hump in the middle, which has an absurd resemblance to the button, and there is a kind of pouch like a sporran. The Kachins resembled the Shans in some ways, but were not all dressed alike. Some of the women had a most odd arrangement of coils and coils of cane round their middles which made them look like tubs, and the same cane rattans were wound around each knee. Huge earrings of silver and chains of every sort of bead were to be seen everywhere. Silver seemed to be the predominant metal. This is different from the Burmese custom, which is to give only the children silver ornaments and themselves to wear gold. There were numbers of true Chinamen about, mostly dressed in the lovely sky blue which makes such a refreshing break in the colour-scheme. One poor little Chinese woman was hobbling about on terribly deformed feet, until I had actually seen her I could not believe in anything so repulsive and hideous. I had always expected to see the feet compressed indeed, but larger and not so gruesomely distorted. The people were squatting in rows on the ground beside their wares, mostly contained in great baskets, and they looked at me with interest but without undue curiosity.

I noticed a surprising number of cases of goitre, which is odd, as these people, like the Swiss among whom it is most prevalent, live in the hills, but in their case it can hardly be from the drinking of snow water, which is said to be the cause of the disease in Switzerland. Another unpleasant detail is the number of teeth stained and blackened with kutch, which is as universally chewed up here as betel-nut further south. Mr. E. explained to me the various edibles that were for sale ; a great dish of saffron, the colour of poongyis' robes, was for curry ; a mass of dirty-looking sand was flour and peppercorns ground together ; and most common and most sickening of all was the national food n'gape (pronounced nappy). I saw enough of this in Bhamo and smelt enough of it to make me remember it all my life. Piled on the plank floors of the living rooms, open to the street, in one house after another, I saw heaps of the decaying fish which are left until they attain that state of decomposition which makes them most toothsome to the strong-tasting Burman. In the meantime dust and sand, to say nothing of microbes, must have penetrated every pore of the filthy mass, which is then pounded up and used for food. In the market this delicacy, with others, was dealt out on broad bits of plantain leaf which served equally for a plate or a wrapping.

Besides the local foods there were great baskets of walnuts, nuts, dried figs and many other things. After seeing the market we went on to the joss-house. It is surrounded by a high wall and contains innumerable courts, not set square to each other, but opening at various angles, probably for the greater show of mystery. In one court near the entrance there is a theatre, not with the stage, as one might innocently suppose, on the ordinary level, but high up on the flat place above the entrance, so that only the people sitting in the galleries round the court could see anything going on, those in the well of the court could see nothing. Everywhere was the distinctive carving and painting of the Chinese, but the place looked worn and poor, not well kept and bright. The building is of considerable antiquity in parts. All the roofs had the characteristic round Chinese tiles running down in ridges. In one place a shrine, so sacred as to be shut off by folding doors, had spread before it an old carpet which had belonged to the Irrawaddy Flotilla Company, whose name was still prominently woven in it ! On each side was a hideous devil, before which burnt a bowl of saffron. Biscuit boxes with tapers stuck in

them were placed before other figures, which, life-sized
and gilt, made a kind of frieze. We saw many slow,
dull-looking Chinamen lolling about in the courts, but
no one seemed to resent our presence there in any way.
We afterwards walked through China Street; here
there were good shops, all very neat and clean. The
Chinamen had shrewd, clever faces, and in their blue
clothes and funny little caps with a red button on the
top were decidedly attractive. In common with many
people who know nothing about them, I had always
had rather a prejudice against the Chinese, a prejudice
which the specimens of the race I saw in Burma did
much to remove. The intelligence, capability and self-
respect written on their faces, and the shrewd twinkle of
humour in their narrow eyes impressed me most favour-
ably. They were also much taller and stronger physi-
cally than I had expected, more manly altogether; and
the opinion of those who deal with them is that, though
they will try to get the best of you, as is but natural,
yet if they make an agreement they stick to it honour-
ably. Mr. E. asked one Chinaman whom he knew if
I might go into his house; permission was readily granted
and we passed down a narrow kind of alley or entrance
to a very small room, open in the front, but otherwise
unlighted, filled with costly furniture; lacquer and
gilding and inlaid work met my eyes everywhere; the
whole was the exact antithesis of the large bare
unfurnished rooms of the wealthy Burmese. The
owner pointed with pride to numbers of strips of red
paper suspended on strings from the ceiling as if they
were put there to dry, and Mr. E. explained that these

THE "INDAW" (*p.* 172)

FISHERMEN

were all greetings from his friends at the Chinese New
Year, which begins in April when the sun enters Aries.
The old man was evidently very proud of them, for he
smiled with a pleased expression at my evident astonish-
ment. Only second to his " greetings " did he value
his goldfish, which were in a bowl outside the door; I
thought him pleasant and civil, but nevertheless the
feeling of racial difference is far wider and deeper
between English and Chinese than between English
and Burmese.

There is one shop by way of being a store in Bhamo,
and here I went to get what I should need for the trip
up the river. There was nothing on the launch except
a couple of benches and a wooden table; but, as it
would have been absurd to buy such things as crockery
for two days' use, I was told that I could borrow most
of what I required from the dâk bungalow, and need
only get food, oil for the lamp, and other goods of a
perishable kind at the store. I had given the boy
orders to go to the bazaar and buy what I should need
in the way of eatables for two days, and he brought me
a list with such strange items as " ghi " in it. He
seemed to know very well what quantities to get and
was most helpful. Though his list included chickens,
rice, beef, bread, vegetables, &c., it only amounted to
a few rupees in all. Jam, biscuits, soda water, knives
and forks, and smaller things, to say nothing of a tweed
cap for comfortable wear, I managed to procure at the
store, but the process was prolonged. The only man
who knew where anything was or what the price of
anything happened to be was the owner, and he did

Y

not seem greatly interested; besides, as while I was there my friend the engineer with one or two of his assistants was trying to obtain supplies for a journey which might extend over a couple of months, my small purchases fell into the background. There were two assiduous natives who would have been willing enough to get me anything they could, but as they had not the faintest idea what I wanted, and if they had, would not have known whether they had it, or where to have found it, we did not get on very fast. I managed to buy two enamel plates that I thought might be useful; these were afterwards the glory and delight of Chinnasawmy's life, he looked on them with covetous eyes, and at last one day managed to break through the desperate reserve of a native, to ask if I intended to take them back to England. When I told him no, I should leave them as a legacy for him, his solemn face became quite radiant, and he said the word "Thanks," very unusual for a native. To return to the store: I found the only way was to hunt for oneself in the hope of finding anything likely, and managed thus to rummage out one or two items, and, ordering the medley to be sent up, I retired.

I had a pleasant surprise while in Bhamo in coming across a lady I had met in Rangoon, and she called on me that same afternoon and carried me off to tea; when you have lived even for a short time on the ever-same toast with the smoky taste, English bread and butter and home-made cakes are a treat. The garden was full of flowers, roses and violets, and great sprays of waxy orchids, but it is unfortunate that English flowers seem

to lose their smell out here; the roses have rather a
sickly scent, and are generally of the pale pink or white
variety, one rarely sees a deep rich-coloured rose. Yet
with many difficulties and drawbacks it is wonderful
how charming and home-like some people manage to
make their bungalows. After tea we drove round the
circular drive and I went home, made happy by the loan
of a mattress to soften the benches on the launch,
benches with which my friend Mrs. A. was well
acquainted !

CHAPTER X

THE UPPER DEFILE

LIGHT swathes of mist were still hanging over the wide expanse of soft sand at eight o'clock the next morning when a slow bullock-cart ploughed its way down to the river. The native driver, wrapped in a bath-towel, crouched shivering in a heap on the pole between his beasts, and prodded first one broad back and then the other with cries of " Hoo! hoo!" as they lumbered along. In the bullock-cart I sat on a rolled-up mattress with all my worldly impedimenta around me, including a lamp, crockery, a large coolie basket containing potatoes and various other things, and three skinny little live chickens tied by the legs. Their cramped position and lack of plumpness made me so unhappy that I stipulated that those intended for the morrow should at least be fed during the day. Trudging after me, ankle-deep in sand, came Chinnasawmy with a bottle of oil in one hand and an enamel basin, my sole washing-stand crockery, in the other.

The little launch *Indaw* was waiting when I reached the river, and as I walked up the plank the serang, with his silver chain of office around his neck, salaamed humbly. I went forward and found a wee deck space just enough to hold the deck-chair Mr. E. had lent me close beside the wheel; then the boy came flying wildly to me with great anxiety on his countenance: " Missie, no cooking-pots!" Now the Deputy Commissioner's wife, who had kindly offered to lend me her cooking-pots, had told me she had sent them down the night before and that they had been placed on board. I told Chinna to look again to make sure that there was no mistake, but further search confirmed the fact that they were missing. Several days afterwards when I was returning on the " ferry " steamer a soiled bit of paper with my name on it and nothing else was handed to me, and after puzzling over it for long I solved the mystery, jumping to the correct conclusion that the cooking-pots had been put on the " ferry " steamer instead of the launch by the coolie who had brought them down. The boy had to hurry back to borrow the pots from the dâk bungalow, and I sat meantime and surveyed the cold waste of water while the serang fretted, for if we wished to get through the dangers of the defile before nightfall we should have been off as soon as the mist lifted. In about forty minutes Chinnasawmy returned trium-phantly, and immediately afterwards we got under way.

The morning was very grey indeed and the sky covered with clouds. Long, low-lying sandbanks were all the scenery at present available, and I was thankful for my big fur coat. We skirted close in by the shore at first, along banks covered with coarse elephant grass, and passed huge half-submerged rafts of logs, mostly with funny little huts in the middle, in which the natives who went down the river lived. Over one, hundreds and hundreds of crows were wheeling and screaming with a horrible persistence, and at last out of the thatch hut rushed a very wild-looking man with a stick and beat at them in impotent fury. I wondered what lay hidden beneath that thatch ! Along the shore at intervals were curved bamboos bent down over the water and connected with a kind of triangular arrangement. I knew they were for fishing, but could not understand how they worked. Here and there we passed odd high-prowed boats, whose owners gathered to stare at us. I could always judge from the amount of attention I received whether white people were rarities or not in any particular district. The hills in front were enwrapped in clouds almost to the peaks, which stood out above like sharp detached islands. I asked the boy to inquire of the serang if it might remain grey all day or if the sun always came out, and was assured, comfortingly, that the sun always came out, an assertion that unfortunately failed of justification. At eleven o'clock I had breakfast ; it was the first time I had been at the mercy of the boy's cooking and I found it admirable—a poached egg, a nice little bit of beef done up with all sorts of savoury vegetables, and curried chicken.

I could not read or write at all as the hours sped by, everything was too fascinating and novel. I sat most of the time within a few inches of the man at the wheel, near whom the serang stood. He was continually on the watch, for the sandbanks change and shift with alarming rapidity, and it needs long acquaintance with the river to avoid danger; sometimes at the word of command the wheel was swung almost round at the last minute to avoid a shoal, and sounding went on perpetually in primitive fashion with bamboos. I had plenty of time to admire the dignity of the serang in his blue linen costume and little round cap. His trousers were made on the opposite principle to a costermonger's, baggy at the knee and so tight at the ankle the mystery was how ever he got into them. Though neither he nor any one else of the native crew spoke any English, yet oddly enough the words of command about the steering were given in English.

By twelve o'clock we were fairly in the defile, the longest and most beautiful of the three. In some ways the scenery reminded me of Scotland, and it was only the nearer views, when the differences in foliage could be noted, that destroyed the illusion. Great wooded hills rose in all directions, and the feathery trees grew right down to the water's edge, with here and there breaks and little bays of glistening white sand. The channel was extremely tortuous, with headlands projecting into it from both sides, and folding softly into one another in perspective. The chief feature in the forest were the masses of young bamboos, which grew like tree-ferns, or gigantic ostrich feathers, with great curling fronds ; they were bright yellow in colour, so that every now and again one had the illusion of a patch of sunlight to break the monotony of the grey day. They covered the hill-sides thickly, and seen against the misty distant blue and the nearer dark masses of evergreens were very charming. I am told that in the rainy season the place is ablaze with begonias, but when I was there no flowers were to be seen. As we progressed we came upon great masses of limestone rock all over the channel ; sometimes it looked as though they completely barred our course, and in one place we seemed to be running flat up against a precipice of grey crag only to turn abruptly at right angles at the last minute. These rocks took various shapes, and it was not difficult to imagine recumbent elephants and crouching tigers and grinning human faces among them. The water was so clear and smooth that every line was reflected, and all the rocks were doubled. Yet the current was very swift, for above the defile the river is half a mile wide, while in many places here it was certainly not more than fifty yards, even counting the smaller channels into which it was broken up.

Sometimes when there was no sign at all of human dwellings, even of the roughest sort, I caught a movement behind a stone, and saw a wee brown face watching me with bright eyes, or a little brown imp like a monkey would spring across the steep sandy bank and run along, keeping level with the launch to see this strange new thing. Once or twice odd creatures, who might have been either men or women, with lank black hair flowing wildly, skipped and leaped along the rough stones, and as I was wearing a man's tweed cap and a big overcoat they must have been as much puzzled about my sex as I was about theirs. The dug-out canoes were to be seen pretty frequently. These boats are really worth a good deal, rough-looking as they are, for they must all be in one piece, and the tree that furnishes forth length and

WAITING FOR THE STEAMER AT
MODAH, BELOW BHAMO

THE UPPER DEFILE, IRRAWADDY

girth enough is a fine one. Such a tree is valuable, and permission has to be obtained before it can be cut down. It costs money. The hollowing out is also a considerable affair. Whenever possible these wild people are subjected to a hut tax, but very little is yet known of them. One has only to read such a book as Sir J. G. Scott's *Burma, a Handbook*, to find out how much there is still to learn. In one place he says:

"The Hpön are a small community in the hills along the Irrawaddy near and below Sinbo. In speech they might be either Burmese or Shan. They have long been isolated in the hills along the upper defile, which offered no attractions to anybody. They are a kind of lees or scum of the neighbourhood, and possibly were in the beginning refugees from justice or from tyranny." I like to think some of these odd wild animal-like creatures I saw were Hpön.

I found that the serang was aiming at a small place called Sinbo, but I began to doubt if we should make it, our progress was so slow. I had tea about five. It was still grey, grey all day, the one completely grey day I had in Burma, and this seemed a pity, for though it was sunny when I returned the defile is not seen nearly so well coming down; besides, the launch goes much faster, so as to leave less time for impressions; therefore my memory of this wonderful bit of scenery will always be as a clear photograph without colour.

At last we were through the defile, and coming into a wide stretch of shallow water almost immediately ran into a sandbank with a swish, a soft lift, and a bump as on a feather pillow. We were not the only people in

z

difficulties, for away across the wide water I saw a boat of considerable size, out of which the native owners had stepped into the water in hope of shoving it along. In the midst of such an expanse, a veritable sea, it was curious to notice that the water did not reach much above their ankles.

We, for our part, shoved off backwards, and executing a wild semicircular movement made a rush at the channel nearer in shore, only to land again with the lift and soft bump with which I was becoming familiar. This time it was more difficult to get off, but we managed at last, and tried again the third time to get through. After exciting sounding on both sides we stopped just short of another undesired landing. The serang called a council of his subordinates, and they all gave their opinions with much freedom and volubility at one and the same time, and I was only prevented from adding mine to the number by my inadequate knowledge of the language. After another try we negotiated this dangerous place, and went merrily for a hundred yards, then again we landed plump and square on a bank, with a thud which made the launch reel. It was a curious situation—to be stuck here under a saffron sky, the pale reflection of a sulky sun, amid a grey waste of shallow water, away, around, behind and before. We were stopped for an age this time, and I really thought the serang was going to cry, he looking so despairing; I longed to tell him to " cheer up." The line of trees on the further shore was quite black ere we finally crawled over the bar into safety. Then there was more anxiety; Sinbo was some way ahead, navigation was impossible in the dark, and it *was* dark, with only the pale crescent of a watery moon to mock us. There was much pole-sounding, and a very cautious advance, until at length a light appeared, low down on the water, and another considerably further on. This must be Sinbo, I thought, for two lights hereabouts are quite sufficient indication of a village. We finally drew in to the bank, and the nose of the boat was run up against the mud. Then the boy came to inform me we were going to stop there for the night, and that the further light—the other had disappeared—probably indicated the launch the Deputy Commissioner was on, for it was quite likely he was in the neighbourhood. I had letters and stores for him, and I thought it was a pity we had not worked up near to him, but I reflected if we could see his light he could see ours, and it was easier for him to come down stream than for us to go up. So I told Chinnasawmy to get on with his cooking, while I cleaned myself up as well as circumstances permitted. It was certainly very very still, not a sound on any side. The little cabin looked cosy with the lamp on the wooden table, and I enjoyed my dinner. Whilst I was in the middle of it a dark face appeared at the window, and a black hand thrust a telegram at me; astonished was I to read my own name thereon! It was a curious chance. Some one had wired to me care of the Deputy Commissioner, and Mr. E. from his office, being the only man who knew my whereabouts, had wired on to Sinbo. The natives are very clever at tracking out strangers, and one had come down to the river-side, and handed it to the only European probably within many miles.

Later, when I had finished, the table was moved to one side, the two benches put together, and my bed made ready. I cannot say it was comfortable. It is in the arch of the ribs that it catches you about four o'clock in the morning, when you are lying on something very hard. Moreover, I found the place stuffy, for I felt compelled to close the shutters of the cabin lest pryers should look in. It was a curious experience, and enough to keep one awake, to feel one was quite alone with natives, and to hear them grunting and making interjections and conversation within a few inches of one's head. There was a good deal of settling down, and gargling, and mouth-washing, but by nine they were all quiet, though during the night I was awakened several times by a grunt or snore so near to my head that I started until I remembered there was a plank about half an inch thick between us.

Next morning there was a dense white mist, but it cleared off, and the effect as it rolled up in what seemed gigantic wisps of fleecy cotton wool was very fine. The other launch, from which the light had come, had vanished, gone on up stream; it probably belonged to some forest official, and the Deputy Commissioner was not on board. As I had been asked to give his mail into his own hands, I began to wonder how I was going to fulfil the trust if he should not appear. So I climbed up the heights to the village of Sinbo, to send off a wire asking for instructions. The serang went with me to show me the way. It was one of the quietest little places I ever came across. There were some ruined pagodas as usual; several men, dressed only in very

HIGH STREET, SINBO

M. I. Bingham

A RED-EYED LEOGRYPH

small loin-cloths, were sawing wood in a kind of primitive
sawing-pit, and a few goats and chickens strolled about,
but otherwise there was no sign of life. The little huts
were thatched untidily with split bamboo, and each was
in its own enclosure with, in most cases, its own papya-
tree growing alongside. But there were many trees,
and the broad openings between the houses were little
trodden, and green instead of dusty, so it was not an
unpleasant place. We found the telegraph-office at the
far end, in charge of a very slovenly but good-humoured
babu, who not only sent a wire from me to Mr. E.
asking what I should do if the Deputy Commissioner
did not appear, but wired on his own account to his
colleague at Myitkhyina to inquire when the D.C.
left there and what launch he was on. When he
received a reply he informed me that the Deputy Commissioner would probably arrive at Sinbo about midday,
and added a long explanation in very Babu-ish English
to the effect that he had reckoned it up so because the
Deputy Commissioner was on a certain launch; if he
had been on another one, also named, he would have
taken such and such a time. When I arrived at the
gist of it I praised his marvellous gifts of observation
and departed.

The day turned out gloriously hot, and I came up to the
village again later with Chinnasawmy and the camera.
The place was more alive this time, and I got some
snapshots of children, and a smiling and pleasant
woman, with whom, through the interpreter, I carried
on some sort of conversation. The boy told me that
the serang said if we did not leave at midday we could

not get back to Bhamo at all that day, as we would not be through the defile before nightfall, and I presently had a reply to my wire telling me to leave the mails with the head-man of the village, and return when I liked. So I sent two of the crew up with the big box, and gave the order to get up steam. We had cast loose and were just off, when one of the natives rushed excitedly up to me, and pointed to a launch rounding the low sand-bank ahead. It was evidently the Deputy Commissioner ! So we waited, and presently a launch considerably bigger than the *Indaw* came alongside, and two sunburnt men in topees, and the delightfully un-conventional attire of jungle travel, greeted me, and we all made friends at once. My things were transferred to the larger launch, and the Deputy Commissioner's mail was fetched back from the village, while he and I went up to wire to Bhamo to ask if the defile was clear. He told me this was necessary, as two launches may not meet in it. Hearing that it was we were soon off.

A more delightful afternoon I have seldom spent. Here, where a stranger is a comparative rarity, there is an absence of stiffness and formality which delights the heart of a man from England. The worst of it is that it grows to be a habit, and one is inclined after travelling to speak easily to most people, only to be met in some cases with a cold rebuff. We had tea early and ate each other's jam and told stories and laughed, as we raced down through the glorious scenery amid the great grey rocks, now all illuminated with the sunlight. The two men—the other was a P.W.D. official—pointed out to me much that had escaped my ignorant eye. I saw the great gaudily coloured toucans, with their enormous bills, flying from tree to tree. I made acquaintance with the diver birds and noted their long snaky necks; discriminated between the two kinds of kingfishers, one very like our own, the other large and black and white, and had the principle of the bamboo fishing-rods explained to me. The time went all too fast; it was one of those golden afternoons that come but seldom in life. We arrived at Bhamo about six, and I resolved to stay the next day, Sunday, there, as I had still much to see, and to go on by the " ferry-boat " on Monday. This necessitated going on board on Sunday night, for the boat starts as soon as the mist lifts in the morning.

I found that M. Davera, the Frenchman who has been in charge of the Irrawaddy Flotilla Company's arrangements at Bhamo for many many years, had courteously left for me at the dâk bungalow a huge bouquet of roses and a delightful packet of fragrant mimosa blossoms like little balls of fluff, wrapped up in a plantain leaf. This very charming form of courtesy is frequently met with in Burma.

Next day early I had a visit from a box-wallah, a clever man from whom I bought a certain amount of silver. The manner of buying adds greatly to the pleasure of the transaction; the silver article is balanced against its weight in rupees, and so much is added to every rupee for workmanship. This man asked eight annas a rupee for Burmese work, and four annas a rupee for Indian work. I found afterwards that this was not extravagant, as a rupee for a rupee is not an uncommon allowance, though it depends on the fineness of the work. We had a pleasant morning's easy bargaining, and I got my silver quite reasonably, for when, by his method he made the article come to twenty-two rupees, I gave him twenty, knowing full well he would not be a loser by anything he accepted.   Among his wares were pretty chains of coloured stones with a gleam in them, for these he asked eight rupees, which I declared was far too much, and when I had quite finished buying the silver articles, he proudly produced a packet of letters which he told me all said "honest man," and drew from them one much worn stating that he was a good sportsman, that he tossed fair, and if you won you got his goods at a reasonable rate, a rather qualified statement, and as I read it he cried : " Toss Mem-sahib, toss for the chain ! "

I laughed.

" Toss five rupees or eight."

" All right my friend," said I. " But I do the tossing ! "

Thinking I was very knowing, I took care to select a rupee that had not two heads or two tails, and spinning it myself won, so I paid him five rupees for the chain. Then he cried once more, " Toss Mem-sahib, toss for little silver chain, toss one rupee or three."

This chain he had previously offered at two rupees eight annas. I assented, and once more won. So I stopped, and as I would not toss again, he said, showing all his white teeth in a grin, " Mem-sahib in luck, Mem-sahib done me."

" I'm quite sure, nevertheless, it's you who have done me," said I.

MEN OF THE MOSSOS TRIBE FROM
THE YUNNAN VALLEY

67

POLICEMEN AT TIFFIN, NAWNGHKHIO

The sequel to the tale came later. When I was in Maymyo a card with the same man's name on it was handed to me, I went down to see him and found not him but his brother. He had the same chains with him, and I asked the price, "Three rupees," said he !

The same afternoon in Bhamo I was in my bedroom, when I heard some one striding about on the verandah in heavy boots, and came out to find a sunburnt ruddy Frenchman dressed in corduroys. As I had my tea he told me he had been travelling in China for eighteen months buying musk for one of the largest and best known of the French scent firms. His mules were following him in and would be here presently. He had collected 150,000 rupees worth of musk in tin boxes. His sense of smell was highly developed ; he said he had smelt the bundle of mimosa M. Davera had given me half across the compound. He was going to Abyssinia next to get civet cat, and when I exclaimed at the idea of that being a perfume, he told me that, though it is not beautiful in itself, it brings out the perfume of al. other scents. Of all ingredients, however, ambergris, that strange product or secretion of whales, is the most expensive, literally worth its weight in gold ; it has of itself only a very faint odour, but gives to perfumes that golden colour so much esteemed, and the slight oiliness considered essential. Monsieur was very talkative, and when I heard he was putting up at the dâk bungalow that night I was not sorry I myself was going on board. Soon after there arrived his pony and convoy of mules, jingling into the compound, in charge of their

2 A

strange, wild-looking drivers, men of the Mossos tribe from the Yunnan valley. Though the light was darkening, I took what photos I could as they unloaded the mules, who immediately rolled delightedly in the dust to ease their sore and weary backs.

CHAPTER XI

A TIGER SCARE

THE next scene finds me far from Bhamo. I had come down the way I had gone up, by steamer and rail to Mandalay, stayed one night at the dâk bungalow there as the circuit house was full, and caught the train the next day to Maymyo, lying up on the Shan plateau to the east. The journey between Mandalay and Maymyo is not long, and for the first part quite level. The line runs by the outskirts of the town, giving an opportunity for good views of the golden spire of the Arakan pagoda, and passes Myohaung Junction, which now seemed like an old friend so often had I been through it; after this it branches off from the Amarapura line, going straight to the foot of the towering hills that border the Shan plateau and form so conspicuous a feature from Mandalay. These rise to a height of four thousand feet above sea level. Arrived at the foot of them I wondered what the train was going to do, as the face of the hill was as the face of a cliff, but there was no doubt or hesitation, no creeping through some gently ascending valley, not a bit of it. We went sheer up in reversing zigzags, and, as the engine was a kind of Siamese twin, like two engines back to back, it started off gaily in the new direction at each angle without the least difficulty.

Higher and higher we rose, looking down on the sections of the line up which we had. come, and the immense plain spread out before us wider and wider, flat country stretching to seeming infinity of distance. Then there came heavy rock cuttings, and we lost sight of the plain, but in compensation could soon peep over the other side of the ridge, for we were nearing the summit. Tall straw-coloured grass grew abundantly near the line and the jungle growth was thick. There were the great white convolvuluses with crimson centres climbing over everything, also smaller ones bright mauve in colour. Very common was a large free-growing shrub, covered all over with velvety flowers, not unlike almond blossoms, but the colour of lilac. The quickly sinking sun caught the hills at all angles and brought out as startling patches of colour the large blood-red leaves appearing amid the green foliage. Then we ran along the heights with huge tree-covered valleys rolling away on the far side.

I had not started till midday, and it was dark and late when I arrived at Maymyo, which is entirely a modern military hill-station sprung up in the last few years. I was met at the station by the very courteous Assistant Commissioner, who had come provided with passports for me and the boy, otherwise we might have had difficulty. Maymyo had been so singularly free from the plague the authorities wished to keep it so, and insisted very stringently on this formality. The circuit house where I stayed, which was much more like an ordinary English house than those I had so far been in, had brick walls, and there was actually a wood fire burning brightly on the open hearth, a welcome sight, for it was quite cold. I only stayed one night at Maymyo this time, going on the next day to the celebrated Gokteik Gorge, which attracts sightseers from all parts of the world.

As I have said, in Burma it is always wise to notify the station-master when you want to travel, or there may be a shortage of accommodation, and there was in this case, for when I arrived at the station about midday on the morrow I found him metaphorically tearing his hair, as no less a party than seven besides myself were visiting Gokteik, some three hours' journey away, and this was apparently an overwhelming number. There were an American and his wife, a Scotsman and his wife, an old gentleman from Ireland, a Parsee and his wife, and all of them had to be fed at the dâk bungalow at Gokteik which was run by the railway. What we were to feed on heaven alone knew! When I advised sending up some extras from the refreshment-room at Maymyo the station-master jumped at the brilliant idea, and I believe a tin of biscuits actually went in the van. Having found that the two first-class carriages were quite inconveniently full I decided that if the station-master would give me a second reserved, I should prefer it, though of course I held first-class tickets. He assented willingly, but this proceeding did not at all suit Chinnasawmy's ideas of my dignity. He could not understand my preferring to be alone in slightly worse circumstances rather than

to travel in a herd in better; in fact, I suppose the
herd in itself would be an additional attraction to a
native.   He came and stood in the door of my carriage
and sniffed, and said: "That man make bill short,
Missie."

I said, "What?"

"That man make bill short."

Then I saw what he was driving at, he thought the
railway company should take off something from my fare,
so I laughed and sent him away.

The train goes very slowly, literally little more than a
foot's pace most of the way.   The line runs sometimes up
and sometimes down, but the down-grades did not make
up for the slowness of the progress uphill.   There were
times when the engine puffed frantically without moving
at all, and I thought we should have to get out and
walk to lighten it, as one might do with a coach in the
Lake Country.   However, the surroundings were to me
intensely interesting, and the delay pleasant rather than
not.   I saw a great deal that was strange, admiring
especially the wild high-growing jungle grasses, and a
tree covered all over with blossom as bright as scarlet
sealing wax, which I learned afterwards was the wild
cotton.   I constantly tried at the stations to get photos
of the characteristic groups awaiting the train, but the
difficulties were almost insuperable.   To begin with, the
train invariably pulled up with the platform "into the
sun" so unless I got out and walked to the far side I
could not take a photo at all; and if I had done that, I
should only have had the backs of intending passengers
for my picture.   Then, when the light occasionally did

give me a chance, I could not attempt to photo until we stopped, because of the wild jolting; and by that time all the groups had broken up, the items were alongside the carriages, and much too near to focus.

On the way back I saw a pretty sight, two tiny children preparing to carry to the train a kerosene tin of water, filled from a ditch, for the refreshment of the passengers. They consulted gravely over the business, and after a long time succeeded in filling their tin from some stagnant slimy pool. Then the elder one said something to the little one, and he, who had hitherto been dressed only in his skin and a few bangles and chains, ran into a tumble-down hut and emerged with a wee cloth, which he wound round himself; conventional require-ments thus satisfied, they balanced the heavy tin on a bamboo, and staggered along on their fat little legs to the train side; as they passed me I dropped a pice for them, and the kindly natives, looking out of the third class near, called to them " Picey, picey." I jumped out, risking the sudden departure of the train, and photo-graphed them as they stood, with their little faces wrinkled in shy perplexity.

We arrived at Gokteik somewhere about three in the afternoon. The station being on the near side of the gorge, the train does not cross the famous bridge before arrival; nevertheless there is a good view looking down on it at the last incline before descending to the station. When we stopped, I, being an old traveller, recognised that there might be a shortage of accommodation, and wasted no time, but set off at once up to the dâk

bungalow which was about five minutes' walk away.
The Scotch couple did the same and came in first,
followed by me and the gentleman from Ireland.   The
event justified the proceeding, for there were two
blocks, one with three first-class sets of rooms, and one
with three second-class sets.   By the time Chinna had
procured coolies and brought up the baggage, I was
installed in one of the first-class sets, and my companions in the other two.   There remained the
Americans, who, I heard afterwards, had been considerably annoyed all the way up that things were not
done precisely as they were in America; and they, with
the Parsee couple, had to settle in the second-class
block.   But they did not give in without a struggle;
presently the man went back to the station, and sent
up the station-master, a little babu, who said to me:
" That gentleman he say you travel second-class, you
go second-class 'commodation, he come here."

I called for the tickets, which had not been collected,
and presented them to him; his apologies were abounding.   I remained in the first-class room.

It is a long way down to the great cave at the foot
of the gorge, and it is best to start at once or darkness
sets in before it can be comfortably reached; not knowing this I had tea and wrote a letter first before making
the descent, and when I came out I found that the
rest of the party had dispersed.   The babu station-
master kicking his heels at a loss for a job was the only
person to be seen.   When he volunteered to act as
guide I assented, as I had not the smallest idea what to
see or how to see it.   The Parsee couple suddenly

68

THE WATER-CARRIERS, WETWUN

Capt. J. H. Brunskill, R.A.M.C.

GOKTEIK GORGE

appeared and joined in, and the boy asked leave to
come, so this strangely assorted procession started.

The view from the platform where the bungalow
stood was superb. The valley rolled away from our
feet thickly covered with jungle growth sloping down-
ward at an angle of about forty-five degrees; it was
spanned at a height of about four hundred feet by
a fairy-like trestle bridge, half a mile in length and
one of the wonders of the world. This, in its turn,
rested on the roof of a natural cave in the rock below,
and as the cave itself was four hundred feet in height,
the whole height of the bridge, from the river dashing
through the valley, was eight hundred feet. The further
side of the valley rose high above the bridge, an escarp-
ment of magnificent cliffs stained red-gold with the
iron that was in them. The railway line, on reaching
the foot of them, slowly crawled up along a shelf or
terrace trending away to the left, and by way of this
shelf it crept on until it reached the shoulder of the
great mass of rock and turned it to continue its tortuous
journey by the same method on the far side.

On each side of the bridge itself there is a parapet
not a foot high, and this is all between the pedestrian
who crosses it on foot, and the stupendous drop below
At intervals on one side are projecting brackets or platforms to be used for the introduction of a second line
of rail if it should be required. Standing on these
the sensation is rather like being swung between heaven
and earth. Indeed, it takes a fairly strong head to
cross the bridge at all, as it is at present but little more
than the width of the single line of rail. Any one is

allowed to walk freely across, and I did not hear of any accidents.

Leaving the actual traversing of the bridge until the morrow, we descended into the gorge to explore the cave. Thinking that the babu was a little more exuberant in his demeanour than was quite becoming, I sent him on ahead and let the Parsees follow to form a buffer. The poor little woman was dressed in the long trailing silk skirts of her native costume, and was further much embarrassed by a pair of new European shoes which made her stumble over every pebble, so, as the descent was very steep, she did not progress very fast. When we had passed a little way down, we could stand beneath the bridge and look up at it, gaining in that way a much better idea of its enormous proportions than from above. It was being painted bright scarlet by Chinamen who hung on, swinging in mid-air, looking like tiny monkeys. The remaining part of the way down to the cave after this was much steeper, it followed little winding paths through thick jungle, from which a strange miasmic smell arose. The path zigzagged round and round, and grew darker every minute ; quite suddenly the babu stopped, and said impressively: " Tiger smell ! "

I thought he was probably tired of escorting us and had invented an excuse to go back, so I said to the boy : " Is he making humbug, or is it true ? "

"True, missie," Chinna answered, his face growing a sickly colour ; " I smell him too, him smell like inside of a Rangoon railway carriage."

Well could I imagine that smell !

The Parsees waited no longer, but vanished like smoke, European shoes and all, and after hesitating one second the station-master went after them.

I was still sceptical about that tiger, and certainly no ordinary tiger would have attacked us so long as the light lasted, but then we were only half way down, and if I went on it would mean coming up in the dark, so after reluctantly peering round the next corner and seeing the same jungly path running down out of sight I slowly retreated. Chinnasawmy had not run, I will do him that justice, but his face was a picture of terror. As I walked back I said to him: "If I had gone on down to the cave, boy, would you have come with me?"

He has moral courage, if not the other sort, for he answered in a very small voice, "No, Missie!" Then, evidently thinking I was angry, he continued in an explanatory way, "If Missie want go cave, Missie get Burman man, he live in jungle, he not 'fraid, he got great big dah, if tiger come he slice him." As I still continued unrelenting he ceased. But as we got nearer and nearer to the upper levels his spirits rose, he hacked at the tall growing plants with a stick he had seized, and said suddenly with a great chuckle, "Them natives, how they run!"

At this I burst out laughing, and he knew he was forgiven. Of course no one ever saw that tiger!

Even if he were not very brave Chinna was a good boy. The dinner the derwan at the dâk bungalow gave us that night was very meagre, but I found that though the others had horrid native-made bread mine was toasted, my butter had been washed, and I had a drop of fresh milk, not condensed, and none of these things had I told the boy to get, they were due to his own forethought. However he had made one mistake, for he had left my towels at Maymyo, and towels of any sort were not to be had here for love or money. We gravely debated the question of the rival merits of my print dressing-gown and my single sheet to serve the purpose and decided on the former.

The following morning the valley was filled to the brim with mist, making it into a level plain ; I hoped it would clear off before the train came in, as I had requisitioned a trolley to be sent down from the next station so that I could run across the viaduct before we left. In the meantime I went down to the station to send off some telegrams. The babu, like all his tribe, was restless, and it was necessary to stand over him to ensure anything being done. I was thus engaged, reading out to him each word of the wire I wanted to send, in a room about eight feet by four, when a hen fluttered in, flung herself on the table, and made the appalling noise hens generally do when they have laid an egg ; I chivvied her out, but back she came. I sent her flying once more, but she dodged past me and landed upon a pile of official papers on a shelf, where she crouched down and defied me. The babu at this looked up at me most piteously, and said, with pathos : " She want lay egg verry mooch ; let her ! " The telegrams were left to their fate !

The trolley duly came as the last wreaths of mist were lifting, and a message was sent up to me telling

CHINNASAWMY AND SHAN WOMEN, GOKTEIK
STATION

71

ON THE TROLLEY

me I could take two other persons with me ; needless to
say it was not the couple from America I chose as my
companions. The gorge seen in the gradual uprising of
the morning mist was even more beautiful than it had
been in the evening. It would have required a Turner
to do it justice. The slow unveiling of the cliffs reveal-
ing each moment long sword-gleams of iron-tinged rock
was fascinating. I and the stranger-lady sat in front
beside the brakesman ; the husband clung on behind,
between two coolies, and we went off down the incline
at a tremendous speed ; there was nothing in front ; it
was like a race on a glorious motor-car ; we simply spun
over the long trestles, and the great crags seemed to race
to meet us, while the clouds rolled up from the more
distant blue hills at the end of the valley. Never have
I done anything more exhilarating ! The Scotch lady
grasped my arm in the midst of it all and said, with the
utmost impressiveness : " How many yards of silk did
you get for those petticoats at Mandalay, if I may ask ? "
I answered, with equal fervour, " Five ; do you think it
was enough ? " Verily there are some people to whom
shop windows form the grandest scenery of God's
earth !

On the far side we ran up with diminishing speed
along the shelf of rock, through several tunnels, until
the coolies began to shove and we gained the level.
Then the trolley was reversed and we spun back across
the bridge to the station, where the train soon followed
us in. It was sad to have to leave Gokteik Gorge
without seeing the mysterious cave, but I assuaged
regret by plans for the future : I would come back from

Maymyo the following week when the moon would be full. I thought this might be feasible, as a lady who had come over in the same steamer with me from England lived at Maymyo ; I was sure she had not seen the Gorge, and with her help we might get up a party and take our own provisions, a necessary precaution, as the fare provided by the railway had been scanty in the extreme, and the price charged was nine rupees a day !

However, like many other castles in the air, this one was not realised. For when I returned to Maymyo I found it was a festival week, with pwés and entertainments going on every day, and no one wanted to come to Gokteik ; so I had to add the cave to the collection in my Museum of Regrets.

CHAPTER XII

CHINNASAWMY AND ALL THAT HE DID

MAYMYO is a hill station; the pleasant bungalows are
dotted about with great spaces of open ground between;
there is a really fine gymkhana club, with excellent
croquet- and tennis-lawns, and a good polo-ground;
jungle has been cleared away to make room for the
military encampment, and the native town is little in
evidence, and yet curiously enough I saw more
distinctively Burmese entertainments at Maymyo than
anywhere else. I happened to arrive just at the time
of an eclipse of the moon, a date which had been
reserved for a great ceremony, no less than the hoisting
of a htee or umbrella on to the top of a new pagoda,
and this was celebrated with many shows and a kind of
fair, which lasted for a week. While in Maymyo the
second time I again stayed at the circuit house, for
the bungalow of my friend was too small to admit of
her taking me in, and to tell the truth I was by this
time so much accustomed to my freedom that I preferred it to being a guest anywhere. Yet I fully
appreciated the cordial hospitality which so many
people at Maymyo warmly extended to me, for I was

made to feel there, more than anywhere else up-country, that I was really welcome.

The derwan who was in charge of the circuit house took the opportunity of putting on extras for every conceivable item, so as to run up his account ; at first it did not occur to me to tell Chinnasawmy to cook and " do " for me, it was he who suggested it.   He came to me the second day, and said gravely as was his wont : " That man charge Missie too much.   I make the breakfast, I make the dinner, I make all the things."

I said, " All right, away you go," and gave him ten rupees to start.   He came again and presently said :

" That man charge Missie too much for bath, an' for lamps and fire.   I do all that work."

I was only too glad, and though he certainly had his hands full he managed well.   He cleaned the lamps, heated the water for my bath in kerosene tins over a fire in the compound, brought up the wood for my bedroom fire, he continued to " valet " me, while he cooked for me, brought in the things and waited, and went messages.   In fact he did everything for me from morning to night.   I had more reason than ever to congratulate myself on my luck in getting him, for two lady tourists whom I met about this time told me that they had got a " travelling boy " from one of the well-known agencies.   They paid him forty-five rupees a month and he absolutely refused to do anything except look after the luggage.

As I have said, I gave Chinna four annas a day food-money.   When we were on the steamer he had told me he had to pay eight annas a day for food, and had no means of getting his own; he added however, "I say to Missie, I come for four, I not ask!" Of course he knew very well that he would get it without asking, but he was not grasping. Once he said to me with a smile when the question of money turned up; "Twenty-five rupees not much money, Missie," and he added shyly, "I *nearly* not come," as if it would have been the loss of his lifetime if he had not. I asked him one day if he had saved any money, and where he put his savings, were they in the post office?

"No missie, coos."

"Cows?" I said astonished. "What do you do with them when you are away?"

"A man keep them, Missie."

"And do they pay you?"

"Yes, Missie, pay very well."

I suppose he made his profit on the calves.

At Maymyo he began his day by going early to the bazaar in the mornings to buy the food: once he told me, rather as a joke than otherwise, he had had to carry back the things himself, as he could not get a coolie. Most boys of his class would have refused to do this, but one good point about him was he had no scruples as to anything being beneath his dignity, but did just what he had to do without any fuss. Before I came East I had heard a great deal about caste and religious scruples which prevent a boy doing certain kinds of work. I knew Chinna was not a Christian, and I was puzzled as to what his religion could be, so I asked him one day. As usual when he was embarrassed the tip of his red tongue came out, and he was silent.

2 c

I insisted on a reply, " Are you Buddhist, Hindu, what ? "

Still silence.

" Boy, you must answer when I speak to you," I said sternly ; " have you any religion ? "

The answer came reluctantly, " No, Missie."

Religion or not he was honest. I had begun right away trusting him with all my belongings, for I felt it would have been absolutely intolerable to have a boy whom one could not rely upon ; he knew where everything I had with me was kept, he had the keys as often as I had myself, and I never missed an anna or an anna's worth. In fact he was much more particular than I was about locking up and looking after things, and the only time he flatly refused to obey me, though he clung terrified to the handle of the railway carriage, was when I told him to go and get his rug out of his box while I went off to dinner at a station, and he would not go lest any one passing should carry off any of the small baggage. He always hurried into my room when I had done my dressing to put away everything, assuring me there were " plenty thiefs about." Once he deliberately tried to give me a fright ; I had left my gold watch on the dressing-table at the house I was staying in when I went down to dinner the night before I was leaving, and coming up to bed very late, I could not find it. I was rather anxious, and looked in every likely place, I thought a native servant might easily have picked it up, and in that case I should never have seen it again, for he could have kept it for years before trying to pass it on. At last it occurred to me that Chinna might have put it in the jewel case in my trunk which was ready packed in the passage. I went out, unlocked the trunk, unlocked the jewel case, and there, below the tray, it was ! Next morning, when he called me, I said, " Boy, you gave me great big fright about that watch," and he answered gravely :

" Not safe leave him, Missie. Thief steal."

He was naturally a truthful boy, and always came at once to tell me if he had forgotten anything, never trying to hide it up. I am well aware he was no paragon ; I have no doubt whatever he took his small commission on the money he spent for me, and I also understood that the "fever" which he told me he had one night was a euphemism for something else ; but as he was willing, reliable, docile, and there when he was wanted, he made an admirable servant. In fact he was born to be a servant ; timid and of good disposition, he wanted a master.

It makes life easy when you can go off with friends, leaving your things all over the place, and saying simply, " Meet me at the station at such and such a time, and put what I shall want for to-night in the small basket, the rest in the big box," and to find it all done without a mistake. I can well understand how men who have lived in the East for years miss the personal attendance of a native servant.

Reckoning up what I should have paid the derwan and what I had given Chinna during the week I was in Maymyo I found that the boy had saved me about fifteen rupees, and I began seriously to consider whether I should not take him over to Ceylon with me when I left the country, as I meant to stay there a fortnight. The two girl friends who had been on board the *Cheshire* with me coming out, had stayed in Ceylon, and I should meet them there. I knew they contemplated a visit to Burma after I had gone home, and it occurred to me they might engage the boy and bring him back. So I wired to them and received an affirmative answer. This was only a short time before I left the country, and when I told Chinna, who had been looking very woebegone at the prospect of my departure, he cheered up mightily. I told him also that the money he had saved me at Maymyo went toward his passage, and decided me to take him, which I think pleased him more than if I had given it to him then and there.

I said to him one day, " When I leave, boy, I will try to get you a good place as butler again," and he carefully explained that he wanted to be first butler after having been second for so long. But two days later—I always had to be prepared for a context after a lapse of two days, it took that time for anything to sink in—he said suddenly : " Missie, I not want go butler, I like best be boy to a bachelor like this."

" A bachelor like me ? " I asked smiling.

" Yes, Missie."

So I promised to try to find a bachelor for him instead.

I was very happy in the circuit house at Maymyo, for my friend Mrs. H. introduced me to all her own friends, and she and others were most kind in taking me for drives, the form of hospitality one appreciates most. Also I was invited everywhere, and practically " had the freedom" of the club. The walks and drives around Maymyo are indeed endless, and what I enjoyed as much as anything was that I could walk anywhere without exciting comment ; it seemed a natural thing to do here where the native town was not in evidence. The jungle has only recently been cleared, and within easy reach are famous rides cut through it, and endless delightful paths. Maymyo was almost alone in this particular, as nearly every other place I saw, even Rangoon, was much restricted in the matter of drives or rides. The chief drawback I found was, that about noon almost invariably there arose a wind which sent the dust flying in clouds along the roads. Otherwise it was not at all too hot for comfort, even at midday. The society was nearly all military, though there is a B.B.T.C. bungalow some distance away.

The up-country residence of the Lieutenant-Governor is at Maymyo and the family generally come here in March, when the hot weather begins. The bungalow is very pretty and much more home-like than Government House, Rangoon, though without its imposing magnificence. The grounds are particularly delightful and very large.

As I have said, the occasion of the festival, which took place while I was in Maymyo, was the eclipse of the moon, which had been chosen as the date for hoisting a htee on to a newly-finished pagoda ; this I wanted very much to see, as it is a characteristically Burman ceremony, but I found it difficult to get any information as to the exact time it would take place. There were other entertainments, such as pwés, or plays, going

on every night, and while at one of these I heard that
the hoisting ceremony was to be the next morning, and
to be followed by juggling.   Then some one said that
the juggling would be about four o'clock in the afternoon, and I concluded the htee would be raised to its
exalted position at the same time.   All these festivities
took place on some open ground about two miles away
from the circuit house, and when I got down there in
the afternoon I found, to my regret, the most impressive
ceremony of all was over, having taken place at mid-day.
There was the htee, in all the glitter of its new gilt,
crowning the pagoda.   There were crowds of Burmans
about admiring it, and the whole place was like a fair,
with lines of booths and stalls exhibiting various attractions.   Near the pagoda was a place like a band-stand,
where the htee had awaited its elevation.   It had been
built up in pieces, each piece being a great horizontal
slice ; these, in turn, had been placed on a frail-looking
car of gilt and tinsel, which still stood in view, decorated
by a gigantic doll at each end.   This had been run
down on sloping ropes to the front of the htee seven
times.   The Burman knows no hurry ; his great object
is, on the contrary, to spin out the ceremony to its
fullest extent.   The htee had been rebuilt piece by
piece and run up a very steep angle on ropes to the
summit of the pagoda, where willing hands awaited it
and placed it in position amid the rickety-looking
bamboo-scaffolding surrounding the pagoda.   As the
htee went upwards a sea of upturned faces followed it,
and the crowd scattered handfuls of rice on it.   The
Assistant-Commissioner, who had been there, told me

all this so vividly that I felt almost as if I really had witnessed it!

The crowd was gorgeous, the people all dressed in their best, with of course brilliant pink as a predominating colour, but one little lady had on a sea-green tamein of satin, and a sky blue silk scarf, and made so butterfly-like a figure, I could not help bowing and smiling to her, which she took as a high compliment, for she bowed and smiled repeatedly in response. Wee girls, beautifully dressed in tiny crimson lyungis and rattling with bangles on wrists and ankles, looked as proud of their finery as little girls do all the world over. Their shiny heads were mostly bound with fillets of gold and were decorated at the side with hanging orchids. There were numbers of bullock-carts covered with rough thatch hoods under which people had travelled in from the country round. Near the pagoda was a sacred column, newly gilt, with pennants and streamers flying in the wind, and a rough erection magnificently hung with embroidered sequin work which had been the seat of honour for the English guests at the great ceremony. At the back of this, numerous poongyis were lying about in their usual sloth, before an amazing assortment of offerings. There was a wooden bedstead among them, numberless gilt urns and bowls, the vessels used for ceremonies, and every variety of eatable, including Scotch short-bread, milk biscuits, little loaves of bread, sweet cakes, sticky messes, pine-apples, plantains, and vegetables. I imagined the wee loaves of bread could not be improved by having had small candles stuck on them from which the grease had freely run down!

Then we were invited to a great shed where the juggling was to be performed. This was the same place where the pwés were acted, a rough improvised shelter, made of a thatch roof of split bamboo very loosely put together—and when it is loose it is the untidiest kind of thatch in the world—supported on bamboo posts, and covered in at the sides by mats. As we entered some of the thatch fell down, making a great dust, and occasioning much commotion. The place was crammed with rows and rows of spectators, one behind the other. In the centre there were some gaily coloured mats and rugs, on which the men were to perform, these were surrounded by an inner ring of chairs for the English guests. The whole of the *élite* of Maymyo seemed to be there, and most delightful was the friendly, generous spirit of our reception. We really felt we were wanted, and that our presence added to the entertainment. Our kind host, a member of the royal family of Burma, a distant cousin of Theebaw, beamed with good-nature; he was royally arrayed in a pale lemon-coloured brocade jacket, and a pink flowered putsoe and turban. No sooner were we seated than trays of tea and cakes, English fashion, were handed round with great liberality.

The regimental band had been asked to play, presumably as a concession to our taste, which certainly differs very considerably from the Burman ideal. The ruddy, clean faces of the English Tommies and their scarlet uniforms made a vivid splash of colour in the gleaming rows of dark skins around. They struck up at once, and when they finished the native band began instan-

72

AT THE ' 'STIVAL, MAYMYO

S. H. Reynolds

WOOD-CARVING AT THE INCOMPARABLE
MONASTERY, MANDALAY

taneously, as much as to say "See what we can do";
producing on the faces of the young English soldiers a
kind of rueful amusement as they listened to the weird
performance of their rivals. The clarionets wailed, the
cymbals clashed, and the pipe shrieked in noisiest and
most attention-compelling screams.

Meantime the whole scene glowed in delicious colour
that made me long for an artist who could do it justice.
The sun broke warmly through the thinly put together
thatch in many places, and threw bands of clear rich
light on the honey-coloured skins of the three men who
performed. They were all Burmans and wore only
loin-cloths of an ample kind, probably lyungis twisted
up, and their active, well-developed bodies showed every
muscle rippling under the satin skins. Their tattooed
legs appeared like tight blue knee-breeches. Their
turbans frequently came undone in the strenuous game,
and the coolness with which they shook out and deftly
wound up their long black hair again was admirable.
Their "tutor," an old man who sat beside them but
took no actual part, had been to England and showed
off his skill before the king. The performance consisted
at first in the manipulation of large silver balls made of
the same material as the silver balls used to decorate a
Christmas-tree, but very much larger. The men caused
these to run over their bodies simply by twitching their
muscles, and caught them in every impossible attitude.
The balls seemed like living things as they bounded over
neck and back and shoulder, and flew from one to the
other, all without being touched by hand. They were
even balanced on the end of a stick. Then two ordinary

small household lamps were produced, and with the same delicacy and precision of touch these were thrown up and caught and balanced. Then balls and lamps were managed together, while the supple bodies, full of grace and ease, swung and twisted until every muscle was in play.

In such a long strain it was impossible that there should never be a mistake, and not less than the real feats did I admire the lightning quickness and response of brain and nerve which retrieved the missed ball on toe or knee before ever it touched the ground. The clown or comic man had one of those delightful faces in which humour is blended with preternatural gravity, and his shrewd keen eyes alone betrayed the vivacity of his brain. All the men had that pleasant, sensible expression one learns to look for in the best Burman type; men of such expression must have good natural characters.

CHAPTER XIII

PWÉS

THOUGH I was only in Burma a little over two months, I was lucky enough to see three pwés, or national plays, all of different kinds. The first was at Rangoon, and was in some ways the most amusing of the three; the other two were at Maymyo.

The first play was a kind of variety entertainment. We drove down after dinner in a gharry to a bit of waste ground encumbered by much *débris*; numerous groups of people were threading their way to the scene. Our gharry bumped over uneven railway lines, baulks of timber, and other obstacles until at last appeared a black crowd of heads outlined against the light of the stage. We got out and passed through on foot, and way was made very courteously until we reached the front. A rough small platform with a sacking roof over it was doing duty for a stage, and two or three lamps, without shades, were hanging down from the top, so that the glare of their light was in one's eyes most excruciatingly all the time. The entertainment is one annually given by the owners of Rangoon mills for their employés, and the owners and their guests naturally have the seats of honour,

represented by a row of chairs close up to the performance. Along the stage at the back and one side
were two groups of men with similar musical instru-
ments; each played for a set time and then stopped
while the other had an innings, a provision that seems
necessary, as the play goes on all night. The way in
which they played against each other, one set clashing
with all their might and then stopping suddenly while
the other took it up on the instant, was most vigorous,
but terribly distracting. The chief instrument is a
kind of harmonicon, sweeping up to each end in a
curve, along which are strung slats hammered by the
performer; the cymbals make a perpetual clash, the
clarionets a discordant and wailing shriek, and the
bamboo-clappers are deafening. The total effect is *felt*
rather than heard. Gentle melodies would, obviously,
not appeal to Burman taste.

The spectators, who all stood, were in the open
without any sort of shelter, which would have been
quite unnecessary in the warm, still air; the sea of
faces, amid which were a large proportion of those
belonging to natives of India, stretched away into darkness on all sides. In the front of the platform, actually
on it, was a row of small children, who gravely and
critically regarded all that went on. They were,
evidently, of a very poor class, with shabby clothes;
indeed, no silks were to be seen here.

The first performer was the funniest little imp I ever
saw, dressed in the tight skirts and short embroidered
jacket of the old court style, with two stiffened wings
sticking out about the level of the waist behind. It

was impossible to tell if it were a boy or girl. Its face was so whitened with thanaka as to look like a mask. The pink silk tamein clung to it so as to show every movement of its lithe body. It sang in a weird cracked voice, one shade worse than that usually heard in English music-halls; but it danced really beautifully, considering the difficulties of its costume. A more self-possessed and radiantly happy little mortal I never saw. When it paused for a moment some one beckoned it forward, and as it knelt perched on the edge of the rough boards, looking like a huge insect, asked it in Burmese its sex and age, and we learned it was a boy of ten. Two rough men who had been sitting on one side of the platform awaiting their turn now joined in and played the part of clowns, and very well they did it; the face of one was a complete study in humour. I had somehow expected the whole thing to be solemn and tedious, but instead of that it positively irradiated fun, and though it was impossible to follow the jokes, which perhaps was as well, the very expressions and gestures of the men were extremely comical. After-wards a girl, a little older than the first performer, came on and screeched through songs in the raucous nasal voice which seems the correct thing, and held a conversation with the clown in which the great jest was to bring in a few English remarks such as " come on " and " yes, yes," which never failed to secure smiles. The audience were remarkably self-possessed, no howls of laughter, or clapping, or anything of that kind disturbed the actors.

The gesticulations of the actor's long flexible hands

and arms were the most curious part of the performance ; every joint seemed to be oiled, a result which could only have been secured by a life-long training.   The Burmese are very fond of twisting and turning their joints, and cracking them to secure flexibility.   The clashing of the ear-splitting music went on all the time in a deafening din, until I almost prayed that it might stop for a moment.   There was some attempt to suit it to the songs, but that the attempt was not highly successful was proved by the fact that it was not for some time after the girl had begun singing that one of the Englishmen discovered she was attempting " Daisy Bell " in English !   This mimicry of English songs is very up-to-date, and only to be found in Rangoon.   All the evening the English contingent made suggestions as to songs, joined in choruses wherever possible, and generally stage-managed the affair.

The small mites along the front of the platform were quite as interesting as the legitimate performers.   One tiny boy, who claimed to be eight, but looked about six, had great charm of manner.   He sat there gravely, tucked up in a bunch, with the feathery ends of his top-knot sticking upright, and when one of the Englishmen handed him a box of cigarettes, he took one with the greatest self-possession.   A Burmese child learns to have a pull at its mother's cheroot before it is weaned.   This little lad accepted a match, struck it with the utmost grace, and holding it lighted, handed the box back, before applying it to his cigarette ; then he inhaled a long breath with evident enjoyment, blowing out the smoke through his nostrils.   After a minute he passed the cigarette round for each of his tiny companions to have a whiff, and resumed it again. Another mite near him, with the baby bracelets of fat still on his wrists, looked so beseechingly at the box of cigarettes, that it was invited to take one. It was so small that it could not manage the match and stared at it comically to discover which end it ought to strike, finally handing it to an elder sister. When the cigarette was alight it puffed away like a steam-engine, but near the end had to express a desire to retire hastily. Its guardian angel wished to take from it the unsmoked half-inch of cigarette remaining, but it vehemently refused and retired still grasping it in triumph.

The songs were succeeded on the stage by something of the nature of an act, a long conversation between two gaudily dressed girls representing a prince and princess, and an occasional bandying of jokes with the clown, whose chief feature was his straight black hair, which he manipulated in the most marvellous way, without a single hair-pin, so as completely to change his appearance. I had grown so desperately sleepy, almost dazed by the flaring lights and stunned by the tumult of sound, that I was not sorry when a move homewards was suggested; we left them hard at it, with every appearance of going on till the morning. If the children get tired they lie down and slumber peacefully where they are, a habit which must ensure their not being awakened even if an earthquake should take place.

The pwés are free entertainments got up by or given at the expense of some one, and those I saw at Maymyo we owed to the generosity of the same kindly Burman

who had welcomed us to the exhibition of juggling.
The huge irregular shed was full of dim shadows when
we arrived, though outside the moon made the white
dust lying on roofs and roads seem like a covering of
snow. Far away at one side was the stage, hardly to
be seen from the entrance ; the floor was covered with
a heterogeneous crowd, many of whom seemed fast
asleep ; and round the sides, as far from the stage as it
was possible to be, were " boxes " in which whole
families of grandees, dressed in their most gorgeous silks
and costly jewels, with their faces well whitened by
thanaka, sat bolt upright on their cushions. I remarked
that they could not possibly either see or hear from
there, and was told they did not want to ; they came
there to be seen, not to see.

Our chairs were at first put in this position of honour
near the boxes, but when we expostulated way was
made, and they were carried across to the centre of the
building, where space was cleared among the recumbent
forms for them. It was no easy matter to get to them
without treading on some one. A tiny brown arm,
with a wee silver bangle seemingly quite detached, really
belonged to a baby covered otherwise by a mass of rugs ;
a dark shadow turned out to be an unturbaned head,
and what appeared to be a mound of bed-clothes
resolved itself into a whole family asleep together. We
stumbled through somehow, and as our eyes grew more
accustomed to the dimness, took in details. Bath-towels,
by no means over clean, were far the most popular wear,
for it was quite cold. Our host himself had added to
his other clothes a rich fur cape like a lady's, which fell

WHAT I FOUND IN THE COMPOUND OF THE
DÄK BUNGALOW (*p. 222*)

MANDALAY SHORE (*p.* 222)

down to his elbows.   Soiled and frayed pink turbans
surmounted the bath towels in many cases.   The owners
squatted in the favourite national position, and in some
cases were so enwrapped in their towels as to look like
pyramidal tubs with heads.   A medley of legs and
odd limbs that would have done justice to a field of
battle filled all interstices.   Just in front of me a mother,
sitting complacently with her back to the stage, nursed
an infant that could not have been more than a week or
two old. Many brightly flaming wood fires were alight on
the baked mud ground, and the people crouched so closely
around them that one wondered how it was they did
not catch fire.   The acrid smoke added itself to the
pungent fumes of the enormous cigars smoked on every
side.   Rugs of good English patterns, warm and comfortable, lay about in piles; every family seemed to
possess one or more.   On one side of me a man who
had carefully placed his two small children down in
a kind of improvised bed, removed some of his own
garments and snuggled down beside them, with the
clothes up to his chin.   It was impossible to move or
one's chair legs would have injured some unconscious
head, and a variety of jokes flew about among our
party, which was reinforced by many officers from the
camp.   "Don't move old fellow, or your chair leg will
be through that man's head.   Oh, never mind, you've
done it now, for heaven's sake don't stir again or you'll
kill another of them ; wait till it's over," and so on,
a rattle of chaff which, absurd as it sounds, was not so
far from the truth as to be without point.

The show was one of marionettes, and marvellously

2 E

they were worked, not only in dancing but with all the gesticulations of hands and arms natural to the trained Burman dancers as well; the wire-pullers behind the rough curtain kept up a kind of screeching sing-song all the time; naturally this became a little monotonous, especially as one did not understand a word of it. As time went on more and more of the spectators took a recumbent attitude, though when a joke was made on the stage several heads bobbed up, which showed their owners were listening. The effect was so funny that the jokes, incomprehensible as they were, became real and the whole scene was well-nigh indescribable; the irregular supports, the gleams of pure moonlight through the roof, the weird fires, the smoky atmosphere, the glimpses of the cold steely night outside, the crouching figures, the clashing and braying of the band; I began to wonder if I were awake or in some strange new world of dreams.

The next evening the play was not nearly so well patronised. It was the usual stage play about a prince and princess, and was evidently not so popular as the marionettes. The previous night no floor space had been visible, but now square yards of withered brown grass and baked mud appeared in patches. The scenery was slung over a rope at the back of the stage, and did not hang quite even; and when any one wanted to see if his turn to come on had arrived he made no scruple about lifting up the bottom and looking through at the stage. At one end was the green-room, where the actors could be seen making-up. There was a weary prologue, all I am told in court Burmese

ORPHANS BROUGHT UP AT A CHOUNG

77

THE ASCENT TO A PAGODA

not the colloquial language, where four solemn men discussed high politics and the affairs of the kingdom in
the play. When we were all much tired, a bored looking girl appeared ; her movements were very slow and
very self-possessed, she made a few gesticulations, but
she spent her time chiefly in fingering and arranging the
chains at her neck with her back to the audience. At
length with a look of ineffable disdain she condescended
to dance, very slowly and deliberately. On and on she
went, always the same posture, always the same slow
repetition, until one's eyes ached with weariness. It
is not in the least what Europeans call dancing, but a
very slow series of steps done over and over again with
a few twists now and then ; the dancing of the mite at
Rangoon had been animated and brilliant compared
with this, but perhaps that is also an imitation of English
habits like the songs. When the performer at last departed, a slow pompous man, dressed in a long white coat
appeared, the excessive deliberation of his movements
made one realise that the performance must be spun
out until 5 A.M. Putting down his cheroot he kneeled
and salaamed three times, then strolled to a seat on the
stage ; another man entering went through exactly the
same gestures, then another and yet another. We were
told the salaaming was in our honour and was not
usually a part of the scene. The four men sat two on
a table in the middle, and one on a chair on each side.
The long white coats of muslin were the usual half-
dress of courtiers in the king's time, and the costumes
on the stage are court costumes. This became so slow
and so wearisome that we ventured to make a request

that we might have the clown as a relief as soon as possible ; our kind host promised he would do all he could, but he said there was a certain order in which convention decreed these things must take place, and to a Burman precedent is a law in itself. At length the men retired, and we prepared to enjoy the clown, when lo, and behold, the same tedious and disdainful girl who had been seen before came again. It was difficult to sit her out. She fingered her chains, turned round, made gestures with her long thin flexible hands over and over again, but still there was nothing to be called dancing. She was fortunately not so long on the boards as at first. When at last she did go the four men, differently and very magnificently dressed, accompanied by one in a cloth of gold representing a king, came back. The king took up his seat in the centre, and the others knelt humbly on each side forming a lane before him. The pwé had not begun till ten, by this time it was past midnight, and our eyes refused to keep open any longer. Resisting the Burman host's pressing invitation to wait till some coffee could be prepared " for the ladies " we went out into the cold blue moonlight and drove home.

I had told Chinnasawmy he might go to the pwé, and when I saw him next morning he volunteered the pregnant remark : " I go there, Missie ; had enough of that ; not go again."

CHAPTER XIV

ON A CARGO BOAT

WHEN I left Maymyo to return to Mandalay I felt that I was setting my face homewards in good earnest; the trip down the Irrawaddy to Prome would take six days by the cargo-boat, and from Prome to Rangoon would be one night by rail; then I should have a few more days with friends before sailing in the *Hereford-shire* for Ceylon, where I intended to stop only a fortnight between two of the Bibby boats. My glorious holiday was drawing near the end, but still one of the best parts was to come, the river trip, which is all that many people see of Burma.

I am not naturally gregarious, and hearing that there were likely to be far more passengers on the mail-boat, which only took three days in going to Prome, than on the cargo-boat, which took double the time, I selected the latter. The agent of the Irrawaddy Flotilla Company told me that as the river was exceptionally low, the larger steamer could not get up to Mandalay, and I must board a " ferry-boat," which would take me down to it. The " ferry-boat " did not start until the following morning, but it was necessary to sleep on board, as it went off so early it would have been difficult to reach it in time otherwise.

I arrived in Mandalay about 8.30 P.M., and it was very hot, but I knew my way about, and felt so much at home there that it was very different from my first arrival, when I had rushed about to find a decently clean spot in which to make my camp. From the station I sent Chinnasawmy on with all the luggage in a gharry to the shore, and myself went and had tea at the dâk bungalow, where the courteous derwan greeted me like an old friend, Coming out I found in the compound the weirdest little figure of a tiny native child, a girl I imagine, who gazed at me with the grown-up dignity inherent from birth in the smallest oriental, mingled with the furtive alertness of the wild creature. It was one of the most fascinating little objects I ever saw. After tea, as I had nowhere to go, I took a tram and went down to the shore.

But oh, that shore! Luckily I had arrived in daylight or I do not know how I should ever have reached safety. As it was I stumbled about ankle-deep in hopeless reaches of soft sand amid groups of natives with mule- and bullock-carts, which kicked up the dust in clouds. The sun was very powerful and my sunshade had taken this opportunity to refuse to go up. I fell over ropes and scrambled out of dry ditches, I worked my way through tubs and bales of merchandise, and there was no one, no one to ask! I could not speak a word of the language, even the name of the steamer was unknown to me, and when I made a desperate attempt to explain by saying I was seeking the steamer for

REFRESHMENTS

WOOD-CARVING ON A CHOUNG, NYAUNG-U

Rangoon, the natives only stared at me. They were not rude, but evidently were unaccustomed to seeing a white woman down on the shore amid all the tangle of ropes, and the dirt and dust made by straining, tugging animals. Yet in a way I was fortunate, for two friends who went through the same experience some weeks later, arrived in the dark, and wandered about hand in hand in distress and perplexity, having as they phrased it the " most despairing time of their lives." The difficulty was that there were several great flats or barges for cargo alongside attached to the steamers, and to get on board at all one had to elbow aside the coolies, cross the plank gangway, and pass through the flat, and I hardly felt inclined to do this without knowing whether the steamer were the right one or not. At length, however, after walking on what seemed miles, but in reality was, I suppose, some hundred yards or so, I ventured to board a flat, and found on one of the adjoining steamers a semi-white man who spoke English. He pointed out the right boat to me, much further down stream, and I returned to the sandy waste and climbed over great pipes and baulks of timber and slippery inclines until I reached it. The natives, who were loading the accompanying flat, spoke a few words of English, and seeing me, informed me " Mem-sahib boy here," which gladdened my heart, as I knew my luggage was safe, and I could change shoes and stockings and empty out the piles of accumulated sand they contained. I went up to the small forward deck, where I was to spend the next few hours, feeling rather dismal; it was stuffy and uninteresting; but I was in a haven at all events.

That night at dinner I had my first sight of white ants with wings. There are several varieties, and this particular sort are like flat-winged flies, not so large or solid as bluebottles, more of the type of river gnats. Because of them it was impossible to have a lamp on the table ; we put it as far from us as we could. The beasts kept up a buzz like a hailstorm, and actually crawled inside the globe of the lamp, gradually filling it up. The captain, a Scot, who had been years in the country, laughed at my disgust and assured me I should see more before I had done. However, he added, I should probably get off easily, for the winged insects were only to be appreciated to the full after the rainy season.

Next morning we were off very early and soon came in view of the big steamer, the *China ;* after circling round her like a pigeon round its mate, we came up alongside, and were transferred. The Irrawaddy Flotilla Company's steamers are extremely comfortable and pleasant. There is a large saloon deck forward, roofed in, but open for the greater part along the sides. A table and deck chairs and bright coloured rugs make it look homely and comfortable. The cabins are of large size, and that which I had was furnished with real bedsteads, not bunks, and had a bath-room attached. For food the arrangement is to pay four rupees a day, a reasonable amount considering the obvious difficulties of procuring supplies. I cannot imagine a more restful and pleasant holiday than to come down stream thus through this fascinating country. The chief delight is the abounding leisure in a hurrying age, you stop everywhere and

80

ONE OF THE "FLATs"

A BURMESE BOAT

never know for how long, it is just a matter of cargo. Your conscience has no excuse for bothering you, for you must give yourself up to pure laziness and simply drift; even the most fussy of globe-trotters would be unable to make any plans, and would be forced into an outer semblance of calmness.

When I first came on board I found a party of high-class Brahmins travelling about in charge of a young Englishman, but they soon got off, and I was the only passenger for the rest of the way, a boon for which I blessed my luck, as I heard that on the mail steamer which had left the day before, there were fourteen people to fill the fourteen berths!

The Brahmins wore European clothes with soft shoes and collars, and looked as slovenly as only natives can in these circumstances. They had their food, of course, apart from us and kept to their own side of the saloon. They all talked English, and it was somewhat amusing to hear them discussing English books. One of them said to another, "I am reading *Pendennis*, I do not find it exciting," and the other answered, "I am reading *Pride and Prejudice* by Jane Austen. It has not plot, I like plot, neither is it a detective story, it is only history." To this critical estimate the other rejoined, "Read *Lady Adelaide* by Mrs. Henry Wood. That book is interesting from the beginning till the end. It is lovely!"

We had on each side of us a great flat with the bows a little way behind ours, and whenever one looked over the side one saw these flats following with a dreadful monotony. I can well imagine their use, they enable a great deal more cargo to be carried. The labour of packing it on their capacious decks is much less than that of conveying it down into the steamer's hold; also if the steamer were loaded too heavily she would draw too much water for the shallow sand-barred river, whereas the flats enable the weight to be distributed; yet from the point of view of a passenger the flats are a nuisance.

To begin with, when we stopped, I had to cross a gangway often encumbered by a rush of natives, push through an unsavoury flat laden with cattle, and go over another gangway before I could reach the shore, and as we stopped only a short time at some places, I did not care to face all this. Then, too, when we were drawn up, I could see from the saloon deck delightful groups of people washing or squatting on the shore, just too far off to get with my camera; if no flat had intervened, I could have taken many a picture from the deck in comfort. Thirdly, at these same landing-places, the flat blocked my view of all the most interesting part of the shore—the part where the full tide of life flowed—I could not see over its corrugated iron roof, and I could not see round its wide-spreading sides. Yet as flats were the one drawback incidental to the cargo-boat and the advantages were many, I cannot grumble.

The Company has had a very happy idea in placing on the saloon deck two huge mirrors at right angles to the line of progress, so that if you are leaning back in a deck-chair you see a series of coloured living pictures of low-lying sandy shores and green banks and blue water for ever passing before you; to sit and look at those pictures all day is occupation enough as occupation goes in this lotus land, and I fear my system will never be quite free from the germs of laziness then imbibed unto my life's end. The pictures were varied occasionally by a line of thatch and mat huts along the high ground, or by the huge rafts floating down-stream or the quaint native boats; there was no lack of detail.

The first day slipped by very fast, we pulled up two or three times at small places, and when we finally anchored for the night about five o'clock, the captain came to ask me if I would care to go for a walk with the first officer, who was detailed for the duty. I was glad enough, for I always felt in Burma it was a little difficult to walk alone. We wandered through a dusty and very typical Burman village, a jungle of compounds and bamboo fences, and tumble-down huts all standing on legs; for when the wet weather comes the whole place is under flood. The village was completely surrounded by a high and impenetrable palisade of thorn which had only certain entrances. Here and there were trellises with large green vegetables, rather like our vegetable marrows, hanging from them, and there was an occasional tree bearing green limes, but the predominating impression is that of thick grey dust in which rolled innumerable pariah dogs, who simply yelled at us, and when one began, the whole assemblage took it up and the result was pandemonium. We came out at the other side of the village on the wide mud flats of the paddy-fields, intersected by raised ridges. It was very dull and utterly uninspiring. In fact I am bound to say that except for the colouring the scenery down the river is the very reverse of beautiful, and I describe it as I saw it; wherein then lies the fascination? Why do I look back on that river trip as one of my most cherished memories? Why does it gleam out as one of the most interesting things I have ever done? Ceylon was ten times more beautiful, but Ceylon has not a tithe of the fascination of Burma.

Oh those peaceful days, so monotonous in their even flow, but never, never dull. The prevailing leisureliness lay around me like an atmosphere. I used to have chota-hazri in bed, and get up about nine. During the morning I read or wrote or watched the ever-changing pictures in mirror or reality. The mirror of the Lady of Shalott was not to be compared with mine, for she saw only familiar objects belonging to her own country and age, and mine were all revelations. A little flag fluttering on the shore summoned the steamer where there was cargo to pick up, and we dawdled across from one bank to another, stopping at all the little places on the sandy shores. Sometimes I went for a stroll, but it was generally too hot, and then I never knew how long we should remain at any particular place—it might be an hour, but it might be only half—and in the delicious state of my indolence to do anything up to time was positive torture; so more often I sat under the shade of my awning and watched the people from that sweet shelter. At eleven o'clock came breakfast, and by one it was time for a siesta. Afternoon tea was over by four, by which hour we were generally anchored for the night, so it was quite safe to go and potter on the beach and take photos. Yet even at four it was amazing to feel the power of the sun, which seemed to strike down with the force of physical blows.

After the first evening I suggested to the captain I should join him in a walk instead of bestowing my company on his junior officer, and he acquiesced. This was serious business. We put on our strongest boots and I my shortest skirts, because of the unutterable dust and the prickly thorns, and we strode off inland it might be three miles or more, round about the villages, over the waste ground, and back as the sun fell, ready for a comfortable bath before dinner. This was not the last time we went, and during these walks I learned much that interested me, and never failed to get all sorts of odds and ends of information out of my companion, who, like most captains, had a watchful eye.

At dinner he and the officer joined me, and stayed on talking while we enjoyed our cigarettes and coffee, and I learned the intricacies of shoals and cargo. This could not last long, because after a certain hour we had a visitation of the winged white ants I had been promised, and they were much more terrible than those I had seen already. We did not meet them at once but some way down the stream, and the first I knew of them was when the captain called out to me to come and see a sight on the lower deck. A sight indeed it was! The whole place was like a snowstorm—a stage snowstorm—for the flakes flew in a thick white whirl. It would have been quite impossible to stand in it; the insects were not only round the lamps, but in every cubic yard of space, large whitey-drab creatures like big moths. I exclaimed, and wondered they did not come

up on to my deck as well, but I spoke too soon ; a few
of the most enterprising discovered the lamps there, and
five minutes after the place was awhirl with them.   I
could not even have dashed in among them to get book
or paper. They filled me with a peculiar loathing. And
when the vanguard appeared, as they did thereafter
about ten minutes past nine every night, I fled to my
bed and the protection of my mosquito-curtains.   In the
morning they lay like wisps of cotton all over the place,
and had to be swept up.   They then seemed to be of the
same texture as the skeleton leaves children pull out of the
moist earth—all substance was gone, and the bows of the
flats were covered with them as it were with grains of rice.
The captain told me that at certain times of the year
they come out of holes, where the ordinary white ants
live, and the crows seem to know beforehand when they
are coming.   Once he saw two old crows standing
guarding a hole, and presently there emerged first a
few winged ants, and then more and more in clouds, and
the crows snapped them up until they nearly burst, but
could, of course, only dispose of about one per cent.

   Though the Burmese villages were not attractive at
close quarters, they looked very pretty from the river,
and especially in the evening light.   There might be one
or two high-sterned boats, with most wonderful and
elaborate wood-carving, black with age, forming a panel
The steersman sat in a little look-out station, raised even
higher than the stern, and had a roof-mat to protect him
from the sun.   Occasionally, for instance to get past us
as we lay in-shore, four fine bronzed figures would pull
at the oars in graceful, athletic poses, and perhaps so

many as five or six of these fascinating boats would come
slowly past us in a line. But the method of progression
is generally by poling, and the difficulty is to hit the
happy medium, to keep sufficiently in the shallow parts
for the poles to be used effectively and yet not to run
aground. The boats are being gradually given up, because their build and shape is not the most convenient
for carrying cargo, as I can well believe. Once I
crawled into one which was tethered by the shore, having
sent the boy previously to ask permission, and I found
the owner, a rather grumpy old Burman, squatted under
his very low roof smoking. The hold was much deeper
and more capacious than I had imagined, but the work
of getting stuff in and out must be very laborious.

One small oft-repeated detail on board the *China*
which never failed to interest me was the carrying of the
line ashore when we tied up. Eight of the Lascars had
this job under their peculiar care, and they used to swim,
often a fair distance, carrying the line with them to make
the head of the steamer fast to a tree or post. Again and
again I tried to get a snapshot at them as they jumped
into the water, but always failed. They frequently leaped
" into the sun," which made it impossible. At other
times it was too late in the evening, or the shadow of the
boat was over them, so that though I was ever on the
look-out I never got a good photo, and the only one I
managed to take at all was a fraction of a second too
slow, and the movement resulted in a blur. These men
wore blue linen trousers fastened round the waist, and
though they were in and out of the water all day I do
not suppose they ever changed, as the hot sun soon

dried up the moisture. They always sprang feet first, which gave them a bad send-off, and they swam hand over hand, more in the fashion of a dog than a man.

The course of the river, where navigable, is buoyed by long bamboo poles painted red and white, and black and white, these are attached to buoys beneath the water, and they rise and dip and turn with the current so as to look exactly like the necks of swan. I was at first often deceived by them, imagining some graceful bird was paddling ahead.

At most of the villages where we stopped in the evening there were whole families bathing together, father and mother and children; the parents washed themselves assiduously, shaking out their long black hair, and then the mothers scrubbed the babies all over, while the older children sported like young sea-lions. Both sexes were always most scrupulous in their manners, and never appeared out of the water unclad. The women would discard their small linen jackets, and draw the lyungis up to their armpits, fastening them with a subtle twist, then when the washing was completed—and real washing it was, though they never used soap—they would step out on shore and slip a clean, dry lyungi over their heads letting the wet one drop off beneath at the same time. There was no drying necessary. Subsequently they washed the discarded lyungi, beating it out upon the stones; then men and women alike, stooping down, just brushed the surface of the water aside, and drank from their hands; last of all chatties were filled and carried away for household consumption. So far as I could see the invariable routine was never departed from; first they

LASCARS JUMPING OVERBOARD TO LAND THE LINE

83

GIRLS CARRYING CHATTIES, NYAUNG-U

washed themselves, then their clothes ; then they drank,
and finally carried up water for their use ! I suppose
long custom has made them immune from typhoid.
The water was of course running, but it was a slow and
muddy flood, and it always appeared a matter of perfect
indifference to the people if the whole of their neighbours
were bathing above them. The children enjoyed the
performance with a zest that was infectious. I used to
see small girls dancing into the water, with babies
almost as big as themselves, and going nearly out of
their depth ; the wee things, which had cried as the cold
water first struck them, becoming infected by their sisters'
merriment, soon shouted aloud in glee. Most industrious
too were the small girls in carrying the red chatties full
of water up the steep sand or mud cliffs. I saw one
little mite going backwards and forwards with her
chatty many times, though to lift it when full always
proved a staggering job. The river was low as it was
the dry season and we were not able to come right up
to some of the large places as I should have liked, but
generally stopped at a recognised landing or steamer
ghaut some miles off, where there was a small village
or settlement only.

It was a pretty sight to watch the villages in the
evening with the rich yellow westering sun flooding all
over them. Generally there were the picturesque roofs
of the choungs appearing above a grove of palms ; a few
little thatch huts turned end on, or at any angle along
the higher ground ; people gay in their red lyungis
dotted up and down the sandy shore, bringing droves of
bullocks, the colour of Jersey cows, down to water. It

2 G

was odd, too, to see the difference in habits between the bullocks and the great buffaloes ; the former only drank and never went more than knee-deep into the flood, the buffaloes went in right up to their necks in droves, with their huge branching horns making a tangle on the surface of the water. Yet interesting as they were all these Burmese riverside places were utterly different from my anticipatory picture. I had imagined a firm yellow smooth beach like those of some English seaside places, dainty little maidens in pink silk with shining heads and gaily coloured paper parasols, tripping down all spotless and entrancing. The reality was baked mud, dust, good-tempered, rough, coolie girls wearing old weather-stained cotton lyungis, and in the day-time all the glare, bustle and heat of heavy work done under a baking sky, and a general litter of untidiness on the beach. Everything looked much the best in the evenings, and then at a distance ; to investigate the picture closely was to lose the chief effect.

Often and often I regretted not being able to speak to the people in their own tongue, for, as every one knows who has tried it, to talk through an interpreter, himself not very fluent, to people who are shy to begin with, produces but small result. Not only on shore, but on the steamer itself, when I walked through the long covered after-deck and saw the passengers squatting about among all their household gods, I would have given anything to chat with them, but all that I could do was to nod and smile, and nodding and smiling very soon become insipid.

84

AT EVENING TIME, MINGUI

EVENING TOILET, MAGWÉ

CHAPTER XV

THE CHARM OF THE IRRAWADDY

I HAVE so far kept to the general aspect of the river and its villages, but there were many details which are too interesting to pass over cursorily. The first thing that attracted my attention after leaving Sagaing was the junction of the Chindwin with the Irrawaddy; the mouths of the two rivers are so wide and the banks so flat that they do not form any very striking scene, but yet the views were fine seen in full sunlight; the sand was a bright yellow, and the water a lovely blue, while the distant ranges of low heights took on a peculiar pinkish tinge that I soon grew to recognise. Popa, the only outstanding hill in this part, is of volcanic origin, and rises to nearly five thousand feet sheer from a level plain. He is a conspicuous object all along the river for many miles, and owing to the curves of the channel he appears to be first on one side and then on the other. Pakkoku was one of the earliest places where I went ashore, braving the obstacles that lay in the way. I passed through two flats, one beyond the other, of which the shiny iron floors were made more slippery by the occupation of countless bullocks. Coolies were rushing hither and thither with loads, and it was by no

means easy to get a clear moment to negotiate the long
planks of the gangways that swung alarmingly. I
climbed up the dry baked mud of the shore, which
Chinnasawmy assured me was " burning hot " to his feet,
and I watched the busy workers swarming up and down
into the entrance of the flat like ants into a hole. A
brilliant patch of colour I thought was a carpet attracted
my attention from afar, it turned out to be a mass of
red chillies spread in the sun to dry.

Very soon after leaving Pakkoku we came to Nyaung-u
which is, so to speak, the river-port of the mighty and
famous Pagan (*pronounced* Pagahn). Bitterly to my disappointment we did not stay here for the night, so I
had no chance of visiting the famous temples of Pagan
of which Sir J. G. Scott says ; " Nothing quite like the
Pagan temples is to be found anywhere else. They
should be seen by every visitor to Burma."

There are many pagodas also, but the chief ruins are
those of temples which one does not meet with elsewhere in Burma. That Pagan was once a place of great
importance may be judged from the fact that the ruins
extend for eight miles along the shore ! Nyaung-u is in
itself interesting but it pales before its fascinating neigh-
bour. It is celebrated for its lacquer work, but I did
not see any, because it seems the villagers only bring out
their wares for display when the mail-boat comes down,
and did not think the cargo boat important enough to
bother about. We were here for nearly an hour, and I
wandered through the village and got rather good
photos.

Then we left the ghaut and went slowly over to the

opposite shore. The river was so wide here that I looked across a stretch of pure smooth lavender coloured water extending for over a mile, edged by a strip of drab sand, and a long range of pagodas of varying heights and shapes presenting somewhat the aspect of a forest of fir-trees. The chief outstanding objects were a tall golden spire and the white sides of the temple called Gauda Palen, which, though not large, is conspicuous, being near the water's edge. The chief of all the temples is the Ananda, of which I got a glimpse in outline, against the sky. Days and even weeks might be spent by the veriest novice happily amid these magnificent ruins. I put Pagan aside in the nook of regrets which holds also the Ruby Mines, the Mengohn Bell, the "road to China," and a few other trifles.

The same night we passed on to Yenangyaung and tied up there. This is the place of the famous petroleum wells which have been worked for many years; before we arrived I was puzzled to understand the meaning of the tall thin-legged erections like miniature Eiffel towers or the Martians of Wells's famous book which bestrode every ridge and boss of hill. It was the most absolutely dreamlike shore I had yet seen. The cliff-banks rose sharply just like the canvas walls at Earl's Court, seeming to have height without thickness, and were bent in innumerable wrinkles and folds, they were of the same dull drab colour as the curtailed shore, and a few scrubby bushes, stunted and black in the evening light, were scattered about thinly. To anchor here instead of at Nyaung-u was a sad blow, but trade calls for transport and much cargo was awaiting removal.

I went down that evening and walked about on the lower deck to see the cargo; it looked like a hospital ward, for the passengers aft were all sleeping on the ground in rows amid their goods and chattels. It puzzled me how they could sleep at all, for it was tempestuously noisy, but many pwés doubtless formed the basis of their training. The harder a native works the more he shouts, and as there were many great iron pipes and boilers to be got on board the air was hideous with yells. The climax was reached with the advent of one enormous boiler, when the din rose to a maddening pitch, the only thing I could compare it with was a pack of hounds in full cry!

We started early next morning, but had hardly left when we ran heavily on to a sandbank and stuck there. This was our first mishap of such a kind, and as we got off in four hours we were lucky, for a previous steamer had just been on that same bank for about thirteen! The procedure is interesting. After sounding all round to find out on which side the deep water lies, the anchor is taken out in a boat and dropped some way off, and the steamer steams up to it, if it drags you wait and "smoke a cheroot" (I quote the captain), for the silt coming down will soon root it there beyond the possibility of its being pulled up.

The Lascars in their blue trousers, with long white tunics down to the knee, their bright scarlet belts and little flat round forage caps always reminded me of men in a comic opera, for they did a great deal of scrambling

THE LASCARS AND THE ANCHOR

CHILDREN AND PARIAH DOG, APHAN-ZEIG (*f.* 244)

and shouting and getting in each other's way, but never were they so comic-opera-ish as on this occasion. The huge anchor was balanced on one side of the boat ready to be let go, and the natives instinctively and without thought gathered on the opposite side to counterbalance it—result, the anchor went over certainly, and so did the men as the boat tilted up with the relief of weight! It was the neatest thing I ever saw, of course they could all swim, and scrambled back immediately, and the roars of delight with which their comrades on board greeted the exploit were worth hearing.

Up the river, where the natives of India have not penetrated, nearly all the coolie work is done by Burmans; one sees everywhere the tattooed breeches which proclaim their race. Very well-proportioned specimens the men are, and though medium-sized they are so well formed and active that it is a pleasure to watch them; almost invariably their first thought, after working till the perspiration pours from them, is to go into the water to wash. Girls, quite young things, also carry sacks energetically, and even haul ropes, though the captain said that that was something new. The method by which the incoming cargo is checked, is by tallies or little sticks, one of which is handed to each coolie who goes with a sack across the gangway, and the overseer on board collects the tallies for the total number, the workers are not paid individually, but just hired together, and as they come and go pretty evenly this is a fair method. At very many places a sky-blue or black-clad Chinaman, invariably with an umbrella, came down in charge of cargo to put abroad, he was almost always owner or manager, not workman. Between the natives of India who are getting all the rough work and shoving up from below, and the Chinaman seizing business opportunities and making his pile above, the Burman will eventually find himself a bit squeezed, but at present he is quite happy and does not at all object to other people doing his work.

At a place below Yenangyaung, a mere ghaut or landing, with no huts at all, I went on shore for a walk. The country realised my idea of South Africa, the low ridges were simply speckled all over with round stones laid so thickly that nothing could have been planted between them; thorn bushes, wait-a-bit by nature if not by name, grew here and there. The Lascars had all run to a high hedge and were picking and eating something eagerly; the boy told me these were wild plums, a little round dull fruit the size of a large cherry, with a good deal more stone and skin than anything else. They are yellowish-green when ripe, and after being gathered, soon turn a brilliant red, which is pretty to look at, but they are then rotten to a European taste, though they are collected in hundreds for making jam. The land, as far as one could see, was of the same utterly dry, monotonous type, with scrub sparsely grown, a stony surface, broken up by deep nullahs or dry water-courses with steep sides. Whichever direction I went in I was soon brought up by one of these and stopped. The boy meantime got into difficulties with the thorny ground, which did not suit his bare feet at all. I should have thought from long use his soles would have been like leather, but he was very sensitive, and even

A TYPICAL GROUP ON THE SHORE OF
THE IRRAWADDY, YENANGYAUNG

STREET IN NYAUNG-U

on grass where a certain kind of thorn is found I used to look round and see him painfully dancing like a cat on hot bricks.

When we drew up at Zigon a little further down, I expected something worth seeing, for several of the high ornamental roofs of poongyi choungs peered above a very picturesque grove of palms ; carpets of the red plums were spread out everywhere, and the place looked more bowered in green and less hopelessly dusty than most. After some difficulties with dogs, and cactus-thorns, and hedges, and palisades, we got near the poongyi choungs, and found a little group of boys playing together. Chinnasawmy told me they were orphans brought up at the choung. He acted school-master and drilled them into a group while I took a photo of them, and then I gave them backsheesh—two annas to divide among them. It seemed to me hardly enough for about twelve children, but I was told " Buy plenty in bazaar." It is a great pleasure here to see the complete confidence and friendliness among the children. I dare not say that bullying is unknown, but it certainly seemed to me it was so. If I gave the biggest boy in a group any money to divide, the little ones always seemed absolutely confident of getting their share ; there was no complaining, or grabbing, or quarrelling.

The shore as usual was alive with people, but their manners were innately good. They were, of course, extremely curious, and would, I have no doubt, have liked to examine the texture of my clothes, but they never jostled me or stared while I was looking. The motley crowd, all dressed in dingy yellows or reds, were

2 H

seated squatting like great birds in rows, and if I stood for a minute looking seawards and then turned, I would find whole groups of twenty or more removed several yards nearer, but not looking at me at all—oh no! admiring the landscape or seascape just as I was doing myself; another turn away for a few seconds would find them all closer up still, so close I could have touched them with my hand, but still admiring the scenery!

One evening we arrived at quite a large place, which I was told was called Silleh-myo. The shore was most animated, and several glittering pagodas arose from the toddy-palms behind. There were large Burmese boats tied up by the shore, their delicious red wood, toned to the colour of a violin-case, reflected in the ripples of the silver-blue water. Rows of bullock-carts and heaps of merchandise for transport were on the shore. It is a comfort to see how well treated Burman bullocks invariably are. I noted this at the time, but remembered it especially after seeing the poor thin creatures in Ceylon hideously scarred by branding all over their bodies. I strolled off to look at what there was to be seen, followed by the boy and a friend he had picked up somewhere, a native of India, not a Burman. I asked if there were a deputy-commissioner here, and was told, " No Missie, only Myouk; no gentlemens." The chief industry of the village seemed to be in the making of pillows, stools, and mattresses, of which there were piles before many of the houses. We went through the village to a newly gilt pagoda of great size, with a snowy white base. This did not interest me so much as a perfect wilderness of falling and decayed ones behind it. These had an air of melancholy; little paths led about among high-growing weeds and tumbled, rotting red brick. A tall flower, like a mauve and white phlox, grew abundantly at every corner, and dark wooden choungs, with the carving falling to bits, stood here and there. I heard a drone of voices in one of these and made my way toward it, as I knew it meant school was going on, and I wished to see the little scholars at work. It was a poor, small choung, but when I climbed up the wooden steps I came on an interesting scene. Three little pupils were lying on their stomachs, with long slabs of black steatite or slate in front of them. On these they were writing with sharp styles, carrying on a monotonous drone the while. The poongyi, who was an old man in heavy horn-rimmed spectacles, looked most indignant at the sudden interruption, and the pupils incontinently fled into the dark shadows at the back; never had they seen such an apparition as a tall lady in a white topee and European clothes! My self-constituted guide evidently explained to the poongyi that I was a good sort, because after a few minutes' conversation his grim expression relaxed, and when I called out to the children, " Pice, pice!" they hastened back and began vehemently reciting their lessons again, with twice the energy they had before displayed. I gave them the pice, which they grabbed eagerly, and we passed on.

Afterwards, when I asked what else there was interesting to see, I was taken to a compound where a woman was making a strip of cotton stuff for a lyungi. It was a pattern of black and magenta check, and she told us she could, by working hard, do a lyungi a day, but that meant going at it from morning till night. I could well believe it, for she had to count twenty-five threads of one colour before beginning the next, and every single thread of the warp had to be tied separately before she began. She worked the machine with her feet and threw the shuttle across by hand. For a complete lyungi she received a rupee, out of which of course the cost of the thread had to come.

I wanted to buy some Burmese shoes, so we passed to the bazaar, a very poor place—only a collection of dirty sheds. The shoes were all much too small, but I bought one pair of emerald green velvet, and had the whole population of the village round me while I did it. I had wandered about enough and it was time to go aboard, so I asked the boy if I should give backsheesh to the guide, who spoke no English, so could not understand. He really had helped us, and evidently knew his way about; but the boy said no, he was a passenger and only came " for pleasure." I never found the people a bit grasping.

At one place further down the river called Aphan-zeig we stopped for about two or three hours, and I had great fun with the children. I stayed on board, and the saloon deck was some distance, say about eighty yards, from the shore; in this space many small children were bathing and swimming with delightful abandon, boys and girls together, flinging themselves along the water with a kind of gliding motion as I have seen sea-lions do. On the table of the saloon lay dessert ready for dinner, among which were half a dozen small oranges, or limes as they are called here, so I threw one into the water; after it all the young ones went instantly. The

orange floated, bobbing up and down, and at the end of
a wild race a little girl of about ten, who swam splendidly, grabbed it just before a boy about her own age
reached it too.   She swam back in triumph, throwing
back her long hair and shouting.   They then all danced
up and down on the shore, showing in all their gestures
they wanted more; so I threw one after another and
was rewarded by seeing fine races.   The little girl was
far the best swimmer and secured two for herself.
When the oranges were exhausted I asked the "butler"
for more, saying I would pay for them; but at first he
refused, protesting they were "for gentlemen," and at
last, as I persisted, swore solemnly he had no more.   I
knew this was a lie, and sent the boy to tell him so, but
the boy could not get them out of him; he only
managed to bring me one or two rotten ones, and when I
expostulated, saying they were not good enough, he
told me: "Little boys eat this, Missie; say very
good."   Then I remembered I had two or three toys
from the Arakan pagoda—gaudy tigers and painted
monkeys—in my trunk, and fetched them.   When I
held up the first tiger, all red and yellow paint, with his
legs going on strings, there was a yell of excitement
that rent the air, and all the children were in the water
ere ever it touched the surface.   I merely dropped it
instead of throwing, so it was a long swim; but the
small boy who won swam back with one hand, holding
it up over his head with the other so as not to get it wet.
Then there was a monkey and another tiger, and when
the frantic excitement was discerned mothers came
running to see what it was all about, and the treasures

were displayed with much gesticulation. At length, seeing no more were forthcoming, a procession was formed, and the biggest boy, holding the largest tiger high aloft, solemnly marched up to the village followed by all the others, the rear brought up by the smallest who had the purple monkey. Never did cheap toys furnish forth such a royal and to be remembered afternoon's entertainment. One or two of the oranges had been green and did not float, and a tiny fat girl spent hours feeling about with her feet in the mud where they had fallen, to recover them. I had nothing more to give the children but some French prunes, so I went through the flat and down to them with a handful, and was instantly surrounded ; but most of them refused to eat them, not knowing what they were. They took them and held them in their hands, but did not even nibble them in spite of all my pantomime, and one mother shook her head and took them from her offspring. I went back and inquired the Burmese word for plums and brought back an interpreter, an overseer who was working cargo, but the prunes had disappeared. He inquired of a little girl who had annexed several, and found that they had all gone the right way ; once begun they had quickly vanished. I longed for some of the native sweets, which the children would have understood. A great charm about the little ones was their fearlessness. At one place I saw a drove of bullocks rush down like an avalanche, and after them a very small boy sitting bare-backed on a particularly fine little pony ; the child came down at headlong speed and simply flung himself off into the sand, letting the pony go and chivvying the bullocks into the water with a stick, then danced like a mad thing along the shore, so full of wild spirits he could not contain himself. The children never wore any head-dress even under the most grilling sun, and it is a marvel how they escape sunstroke.

The cargo we took in at the various places was very mixed; letpet, or pickled tea, appeared in large quantities, sacks and sacks of the pith the people use in their cigars mixed with tobacco (it is also used for making pith helmets), sacks of dried palm-leaves, kutch, pease and beans, cotton, and when we arrived at Magwé, or, rather, at the ghaut three miles from Magwé, the whole beach was covered by a mountainous heap of sacks. Some one told me there were fourteen thousand! They were all full of monkey-nuts, or, as they are called here, ground-nuts, the cultivation of which is found to be so profitable that paddy is being given up for them. They are partly used to make oil-cake. Of course it was perfectly impossible that our steamer, even with the assistance of two flats, should take on all these, and when I asked the captain what he would do, he told me that the coolies would go on loading as late as they liked, and that he should get off first thing in the morning, leaving the rest for following steamers. It would be months before the whole could be carried off. Like many other arrangements of nature there is a perversity in this matter of cargo, for in the wet season, when the river is high and much cargo might be carried without danger of overloading, there is little or nothing to take, whereas when there is little water and the carrying capacity is limited there is an unlimited amount of cargo. The captain spoke sadly—the greater part of his salary is derived from his percentage on the cargo! It was at Magwé that a slight fire occurred among the sacks, and the coolie girls rushed frantically about, emptying their chatties on to any and every sack they saw, quite regardless of the fact that they were doing a good deal of damage ; there was much more smoke than fire, and noise than either, and the little conflagration was soon got under.

There was a very interesting group of poongyi choungs near here, and I went into the quiet grove around them, and climbing the steps listened for quite a long time to the chant of the little pupils of whom there were twenty or thirty. They could all see me standing sun-framed in the dark entrance, but the old poongyi, who was the teacher, was hidden behind a column. These little scholars were much too clever to give me away, and beyond a nudge to pass the joke on to one another, they continued their loud recitative, with greater animation than before, but as the news spread, and one little face after another stealthily turned toward me with a broad grin showing white teeth, the poongyi began to suspect some side-show and stirred ; so I retreated.

There was an immensely wide road of red dust, a great bund, broad as a river and seamed with bullock-cart tracks, running up to Magwé itself, but when I went for a walk that evening I turned away from this, and passing down a high hedged lane not unlike an English lane, with the boy at my heels, struck out into bypaths. To go with the boy through a lane full of growing things was a liberal education. He knew every

BUDDHA ON THE SHORE, MINHLA (*p.* 251)

BUDDHA BEING DRAGGED ACROSS THE
GANGWAY, MINHLA

plant in the hedge-row. Here were little brilliant scarlet
seeds exactly like ladybirds lying in a pentagonal pod.
" Burmans make medicine," he told me. Then a plant
with dark shiny green leaves like ivy; " Burmans eat
these, Missie." He restrained me as I would have
gathered a tall flowering plant attractive to look at.
" Not touching, Missie ; him got black juice, not good."

Then we came across whole bushes of wild plums
growing rich and yellow, and his face brightened, for he
loved them. I waited while he filled his pockets, until,
as I told him, he had got quite enough to make himself
ill. The bushes were covered with little insidious thorns
bent back like fish-hooks, so picking was by no means
pure delight. Thorns were everywhere, on nearly all
the plants. At last a great black pod attracted my
attention, I broke it off, and peeled it open, and inside
was a little baby loofah sponge, filled with black seeds ;
such is the depth of my ignorance, I had always had an
idea loofahs grew in the sea like other sponges. We
passed by the tall creepers and high cactus, and came
out at last by a great loop on to the main road which
was lined with small mango-trees. Even here the boy
had something to say ; he pointed to two of these and
told me one " not good, the other good." When I asked
how he knew he explained that a mango-tree with much
flower never bears good fruit, and one of these was
covered with the spiky seeded blossoms. There were
many mimosa plants which curled up at a touch and
mimosa-like trees which were looking quite withered,
having drooped for the night-time. Then we passed
the village women carrying up water from the river in

chatties, and enjoying gossip; it was funny to note how the one small boy among them asserted his manhood by carry his chatty on the shoulder, like a man, not on the head like a woman.

When we left Magwé we came soon after to Minhla, where there is the historic fort taken by the English in 1885. The place had an especial interest for me as a cousin of mine, a mere boy, was the only officer killed at that skirmish. The wall of the fort runs along by the river on a height, and is seamed by great cracks, bushes and thick grass crown it, growing luxuriantly, and a mass of dark greenery droops over one corner. No one is allowed to go inside now as it is not safe, and the crumbling walls might fall and bury them. There was an open-air market at Minhla and several pagodas, the central and tallest of which had a golden spire. But the most interesting sight of all was the landing of a marble image of the Buddha brought by the steamer, the gift of a wealthy Burman to the shrine. The image was swathed in cloths and laid on its back and dragged across from the steamer by the narrow plank gangway. Men and women coolies alike left their loads of kutch and flew to help in such a work of merit, and there was much shouting and hoo-ing and chattering, while poor Buddha, looking as if he were strangled by the rope round his neck, was slowly drawn across. The glorious morning light made it a brilliant scene. There were many better-class men come down to meet the image, and they were clad in gay pink silk turbans and putsoes, among them the owner himself, so that the scene was much brighter than the ordinary everyday one.

The Buddha was dragged to a certain height up the cliff-like bank, and no amount of pushing or pulling could stir him higher, so he was set up on end, and the cloths removed, and there he sat, a very dignified and disdainful figure, with the sunlight shining on his smooth satiny arms, while he was surrounded by an eager and reverential crowd. If I had not been expressly told, 1 might have thought he was of alabaster, so fine was the grain of the veined marble from which he was hewn. 1 wanted the owner to sit beside his gift so that 1 could include him in a photo, but he was too big a man for that, he waved grandly with his weather-stained umbrella to others of his friends to act proxy for him while the deed was done. Masses of pickled tea, to be used at the ceremony of installation, were also put ashore, and the festival promised to be a gay one. I wished I could have stayed to see it.

Below Minhla the river scenery is distinctly more varied and interesting than above, and the coast is broken and wooded, and not so flat. We saw many splendid specimens of rafts a hundred feet in length or more, with men poling them slowly up stream in the baking sun, wearing only the merest rag of clothing, but generally some turban or cloth on their heads.

Allanmyo is a large place with many mills, some of them saw-mills, others for making oil-cake from cotton, and the cotton waste, thrown into a brazier, being itself oily, is much used at nights to give a good flaring light. I started off with the boy for a walk, almost as soon as we arrived. The place was well cared for, with street lamps, and wide roads cutting each other at right angles and appearing less dusty than usual. There were several pagodas scattered about, near which as usual the sweet frangipanni grew on brown stems, for the leaves come later. The boy secured me some of the flowers, from which a sticky milky juice like that of a dandelion oozes. In one shrine was an immense figure of the Buddha, and when I went in to see it an old man came up to act as guide. He told me long stories about it, none of which, even with the help of the boy's translation, could I understand, but as he had taken some trouble I gave him a two-anna bit when we went away. He rushed at me so promptly and gesticulated so wildly that I thought he would have slain me for insulting him by so small a tip, so I asked the boy : "Does he think it not enough ?" Chinna's solemn face seldom relaxed into a smile, but it did now as he answered, "He is praying to God for you, Missie, praying, praying, praying, he bless you—he pray you to go to England and come back, praying, praying a great deal." So vehement was the old man's joy, that I could hardly believe all this was for the sake of twopence. " He buy candles now," went on the boy, " he burn them here, he pray more, always pray for you, Missie."

Even as we passed down the street we saw the old fellow beckoning to the passers-by and displaying his coin between his finger and thumb, and pointing wildly to my retreating figure, and all for the sake of twopence ! It was the cheapest purchase I ever made ! There is a great bund, quite good enough for cycling on, which runs from Prome to Allanmyo, and ends in a creek where there was once a formidable fort ; we turned on to this on our way back, but we had walked far and it was quite dark before we reached the steamer. Nevertheless we found work going on in full swing, girls, even quite small ones, carrying sacks of cotton by the light of the flaring cotton waste. I was told that these girls were not paid like ordinary coolies, but so much a sack, and thus they worked fast. It seemed very hard work for such small things, but they laughed and chattered and enjoyed themselves all the time; truly these women are wonderful. I saw one woman with two full chatties, one on the top of another, come up from the river one day and a baby was seated astride her hip!

And then, alas! on the morrow we arrived at Prome at four o'clock, beneath a blazing sun, and I had to say good-bye to the happy days on the boat, days which had glided past so serenely that all care seemed to have floated away from me. I had to turn and face the train once more, and Rangoon, and the prospect of a real and sad farewell. The landing was difficult, across long planks resting on ridges of rock, and it took six men—or so they said—to carry my big box over to the station; as I watched them progressing slowly I smiled to remember that one woman had carried it on her head quite gaily at Sagaing. I always left the boy to wrestle with the coolies as to backsheesh, a plan that saved me infinite trouble, and when they bothered me I sent them to him, and then he told me what he had paid. Native disciplinarians will say that of course I paid a great deal more that way, I might be sure some stuck to his hands. Well, perhaps a small percentage did, but so long as the whole was reasonable, and I took good care of that, I found this plan infinitely the best.

I sent him to the station with the things, while I went to the dâk bungalow there to rest and feed, as the train for Rangoon did not leave till nine-thirty. It was very hot, and I was tired and dirty; I wanted a room to wash in. On arrival I found quite the most dilapidated and tumble-down shanty I had yet seen in that capacity. A mud floor, level with the mud outside, a square table thereon, a screen, beyond which the washing-up went on, walls of badly put together wood, whitewashed roughly, like the poorest settlers' hut, and four outside staircases leading up to the bedrooms above. I asked the derwan, a huge man, black as a boot, where I could wash. He understood a little English, and pointed up one staircase; thither I went, to find at the top on the narrow verandah, a half-caste woman, two natives, and a white man squatting together on the floor. I pushed past to the door, which opened into a dark and noisome room, with unmade beds and other signs of occupation. I went down in a rage, and asked the derwan how he could have been such a fool as to send me there. At last he explained humbly, " Those genlemen not living there, only lady, other bed in that room for you!" I think he was surprised to find I did not assent to this ingenious arrangement. I explained I did not want a bed, luckily, only a place in which to clean up, then afternoon tea, and dinner later. He took me thereupon to the other side of the bungalow, and up that staircase, into a small shed bath-room, of the kind usual in these places; this opened into a bedroom occupied by a white man, who was lying full length on a deck-chair and smoking; it was evidently his dressing-room. The derwan made a frantic attempt to close the rickety doors between and failed, so he said to the owner of the room, who had preserved an immovable composure throughout the trying scene, "Genlemen much obliged not going in there lady washing," and retired. I did manage to wash certainly, but it was precipitately. My blowing-up had done the derwan good; he hustled about and gave me of his best; the tea was not bad and the butter was washed. Having ordered dinner, and the boy having returned, I sauntered out to look at the largest and finest pagoda in the place.

It certainly is a magnificent building, the only one I saw comparable with the Shwe Dagôn. But it lacks the growth, the ripeness of years which so sanctifies that jewel among pagodas. It is too new and cleaned up and much too gaudy. The entrance is steeper, it runs beneath a succession of pyathats of marvellous carved wood, most of it black, from having been oiled, but some a rich red. These have zinc roofs, but they do not jar on one, as the high edges of the pinnacles and parapets hide them.

This fine ascent leads upward to a great golden pyramid surrounded by lesser white pyramids arising amid a grove of greenery upon which one looks down. The situation is indeed unsurpassable. The pagoda stands on a boss from which roll away valleys filled with feathery palms and other tropical vegetation, and the scene impresses one much more with a sense of mystery than does the openness around the Shwe Dagôn. From the platform the hills beyond the river can be seen, and the glint of the blue water between. There are great numbers of sacred bells, and as the people passing round constantly strike them, there is a sweet. rather melancholy succession of different tones ringing in the air. Many of the surrounding shrines on the platform are of the same wonderful carved work as the entry, but there is a difference among them, some of them are really good, others show signs of modern haste and deterioration. At each corner is an ugly square brick pillar of great height, a sort of caricature of a sacred column, and around the base of the central pagoda amid numerous little gilded shrines, are little golden trees adorned with coloured glass balls like Christmas trees. As an example of Burman taste in the gaudy it is especially interesting, and even with all the overloaded tawdriness the mighty pagoda in its fine position is very fascinating. The boy admired it greatly. His feelings were too much for him, and he ventured to say it was better than the Shwe Dagôn. Afterwards we passed down another approach between huge leogryphs, one chewing a tiger in its mouth, a bit of realistic sculpture I had not seen before.

We went on into the groves around, where were many poongyi choungs. These quiet groves, with the peace of a perpetual Sunday lying in them, always pleased me. We came out down a deserted street where the small huts were partially wrecked, and cooking utensils, bedding, &c., lay in heaps in the road.

I asked Chinnasawmy the meaning of this, and was told it was the plague; the people had all been cleared out only two days ago. For myself it was all right. Europeans only in the rarest cases catch plague, and

SACKS OF MONKEY-NUTS AT MAGWE (*p.* 247)

READY TO START

when I inquired if he were not afraid, he cheerfully replied: " Only English make fuss about plague, Missie ; native, him never mind."

Then there was the night journey, the arrival in Rangoon, the few days there, in which there was so much to do and see I had no time to feel melancholy, and then the good-byes, the launch down the river, the big steamer, and that night in my bunk the horrible feeling that I was leaving all the dear delights of a country which had seemed in many ways so native to me that I could not believe I had never been there before. The ways, the. people, the country itself, I knew it all and loved it, and it was like breaking numberless little strings to wrench away from it. They say that beyond all countries you hear Burma a-calling, and it is named the Land of Regrets because people who have been there are never the same afterwards ; there lives in their hearts always a tiny ache of regret for the land they have left.

EPILOGUE

WE passed down the muddy waters of the Rangoon river, the flat green shores grew grey with distance, and Burma faded out of sight. Those who like may stop here; that is the end of Burma, but to me as a kind of epilogue, a softening of the hard parting, came Ceylon, with its other interests and other beauties. This chapter may quite well be skipped, but if it is only to heighten the picture that has gone before by comparison and contrast, I put it in.

My original impressions of Colombo were not dimmed on return. Happy he who can carry the memory of it with him as his first sight of an Eastern city! I spent but one night here this time, going up-country the next day to stay with a lady who had come out on the *Cheshire* with me from England. She had written to invite me while I was in Burma, so when I landed on a Monday I sent a wire saying I would turn up the next day. The address was Mousagalla, Matale, and in the innocence of my heart I imagined that Mousagalla was the name of a house in Matale; little did I wot of the habitats of tea-planters! We left Colombo at 7 A.M. and arrived at Matale, after changing at Kandy, about 12.80 midday. I inquired of the station-master the whereabouts of Mousagalla, and received the rather disquieting reply : " Ten miles away ; five you can drive, but five you must walk."

" Walk ! Surely I can get a bullock-cart ? "

" No bullock-cart goes there, it is up a mountain," I was assured. " But," the man added as an afterthought, " if your friend knows you are coming, perhaps she will send down coolies to carry you up ! "

This prospect seemed on the whole one degree worse than the first.

" But the box ? " I feebly asked.

" Oh, they carry that, carry anything," he replied.

I went over to the rest-house, which I found a much more furnished place than its counterpart the dâk bungalow of Burma, and had lunch, and rested, and told Chinna to transfer what I should want for the night from my box into a Japanese basket, and ordered a trap.

Coming from Burma, everything in Ceylon strikes one as much civilised. There are good roads all over, quite fit for bicycling or motoring. The railway porters wear dark blue uniforms, trousers and jacket, with round caps ; if they do have bare feet and little chignons sticking out behind their heads, that does not detract from the respectability of their appearance. English is spoken everywhere. Some of the rest-houses are almost like hotels, with copies of the *Spectator* on the table, not much older than the copies one finds in seaside hotels in England. There are pictures on the walls, and wall paper. I was quite embarrassed at my first entrance into one of this sort, and thought I must have got into a private house by mistake. The rest-house at Matale is not quite of this magnificent type, but it is well kept. A very decent trap, drawn by a horse which looked like a giraffe to my eyes, accustomed to the ponies of Burma, appeared according to order, and we started off leaving the heavy luggage at the station.

I had been told much of the beauty of Ceylon, and certainly had seen most wonderful ranges of hills coming up from Colombo.

For most of the way the railway runs along a ledge or terrace hewn out of the side of the hill, with great valleys and glorious blue heights to see in all directions. The line winds about, climbing ever higher and higher, so you get one point of view after another. The wild flowers too are very pretty: the leopard's-bane, the yellow daisy I had seen in Burma grew in profusion; and a little vermilion flower called the lantana, which has a berry not unlike a blackberry. was a perfect weed. There was a dining-car on the train too, where one could get quite a decent lunch, a vast improvement on the hurried meal at the stopping-places in Burma. Many of the railway stations were quite English in their neatness, with English flowers growing in them. In one I saw petunias, heliotrope, roses, larkspur, lupins, peonies, and many other English flowers all growing together. But the fine jungle, the tropical plants, the tree-ferns I had expected—of these I saw nothing.

The road we went on to Mousagalla was exceptionally good and not very hilly; we had to stop to pay at a toll bar half way. Then we arrived, after passing the fifth milepost, at a place where a winding path led away amid trees, and pointing with his whip to a high hill blue in the distance, the native driver informed me, "That's where you go."

No sign of a coolie was there. Evidently my telegram had not been received, or my friends were away; the latter might well be the case, for it was about six weeks since they had sent me the invitation and I had not been able to find out at the post-office in Matale if they were at home.

"Can you get a coolie?" I asked the driver. He seemed to think so, and went to a few rough huts a little further on, returning presently with a lean, lithe lad about sixteen.

"Can he carry all those things up there?" I asked, looking at the basket, which was of a good size, my bundle of rugs, and my boy's bundle, as well as my handbag. I was assured that the whole was nothing. So we started. The coolie went first with most of the things on his head, walking with an elastic step, and the boy followed with my handbag. I brought up the rear. We had not gone many yards before the driver ran frantically after us, crying out, "Lady, lady, there's a river to cross, you'll have to take off your ——." Words failed him.

I inquired if we should meet any lions and tigers on the road, and whether it would not be wiser to take a gun, and the man went back grinning. We soon encountered that river. It was not very formidable, as there had not been much rain recently. The boy carried my shoes and stockings and went first, to prove the dangers of the ford. When I saw the water did not reach his knees I followed. Then we began our climb. It was all uphill, and as it was about three in the afternoon that kind of entertainment was not precisely what one would have chosen; the perspiration streamed down my neck so continuously that at last I ceased to trouble about it. After walking what seemed an immense distance, having risen higher and higher, so that the hills across the valley opened out and gave us gracious views, I thought of resting and was going to sit on a convenient lump of dried mud, when the boy stopped me hastily, telling me it was an ant's nest. I gingerly selected a likely log, and a snake glided out from under it! After this I stood, but told the boy to inquire if we were about half way. He asked the coolie, who had no word of English, and the answer was, "Come very little way, Missie; got great deal much more way to go."

I put my back into it and went on. We came presently to a clearing, and I recognised the low-growing ugly tea-scrub, though I had never seen it before. Little paths, always steep and always stony, wound zigzag through it; we climbed and climbed throughout the afternoon. At that time I did not recognise the other products of the estate, the many-fingered leaves of the dainty young rubber trees, or the great bulbs of the cocoa plants. I had these pointed out to me afterwards. Rubber-growing is spreading extensively in Ceylon, often in conjunction with tea, and many planters grow a little of most things, pepper, areca, cardamoms, and coffee as well.

Every now and then I called a halt and rested awhile, and for the most part the springy young thing who

carried my baggage stood meantime disdaining to put
down his load. Luckily a cloud or two now and then
veiled the sun, and as we climbed the views were so
stupendous that I enjoyed myself extremely. Still we
went on until when we stopped for a minute, even the
coolie was tired and lay down on the path beside the
boy, a little higher up than I was. I could hear their
voices talking gently and I nearly went to sleep.
But darker it grew and darker, and at last a few drops
of rain began to fall. It would be too bad to get wet
here in a country where one imagined that fear to be
eliminated at least from the evils one had to encounter.
So we moved upwards once more. At length it seemed
to me we could not go much higher, or we should be
over the top of the mountain and down the other side.
Then the coolie said something, and the boy interpreted;
" Says he don't know where it is, Missie ! "

I contemplated eating the last bit of chocolate I had
in my bag before I laid down to spend the night on the
tea-scrub, but I said: " Put down the things." They
put them down obediently in the middle of the path.
" Now go and find out, both of you," and they departed
in different directions. They returned presently and
pointing to a cliff-like height overhead, said it was up
there, so we climbed again, a last stiff struggle, and
came out on to a clearing, with a lawn of beautiful
emerald green turf, covered with huge scarlet cannas
and poinsettias, in the midst of which was set a
bungalow. My host, or so I guessed him to be, was
hastily nailing up the window curtains in my room, and
he shouted out to his wife, " Here's the good lady, and

she's *walked !* " in a tone which sufficiently appraised the value of my feat.   They had got my telegram half an hour before, as they sent a peon down for letters each day, and he had brought it up with him.   On receipt of it a native had been sent flying down the hill with a bamboo chair to carry me up, but as he had crashed straight-way and we had mostly followed the paths, he had missed us.   When I saw the bamboo chair I was not sorry.

I was quite fresh, and the air at that height was so beautiful that one could not be long tired.   But I was glad I was under shelter, for presently down came the rain as I had never heard it before, and ceased not the whole of the evening.   I thought I knew something about rain, having travelled extensively in Scotland, but I felt that all I had met previously had been but a drizzle, here it was solid.   The blue views, bright in the sunshine next morning, and the peeps between a fore-ground of royal red cannas, were as fine as anything I had seen, and the whole place had a most invigorating atmosphere.   When my time came to go I rode down the precipitous descent with regret, and as I had found that an old friend lived in Matale, I stayed a night with her before going on to Nuwara Eliya, pronounced for some inexplicable reason Neuralia.

This section of the line I was disappointed with, it may once have been magnificent, but the monotonous rows of tea-scrub running over every height detract much from the beauty of contour. Close to Nuwara Eliya is a mighty hill still covered with the primitive jungle, which shows you what the country must have been at

DWELLERS BY THE RIVER-SIDE

MINHLA FORT (*p.* 253)

one time. Nuwara Eliya is very like some parts of Scotland, and it may be charming to live in, but from the point of view of one eager for new sensations it is desperately uninteresting, being entirely English.

When I left I spent a night at the Peridenya rest-house, near Kandy, and inspected the famous botanical gardens. I visited Kandy the next morning but found little to see, and finally met the two friends, with whom I was going to leave Chinnasawmy, at a junction called by the beautiful name of Polgawhela, and went with them to the most intensely interesting spot in Ceylon, the " buried " city of Anradhapura.

Northward we travelled up the new single line recently made, on and on through miles of monotonous flat country, sometimes wide and open, with gleaming, low-lying reaches of water, at others closely hemmed in by wild jungle-growth. The dusk came on and the stars came out. At length, in the sweet-scented warmth of a glorious night, we pulled up at nine o'clock at the small station where we were to get out. We hired a tiny pony-cart, driven by a scantily clothed man with a very honest expression, and all crammed in, leaving the boy to bring the things on to the rest-house by bullock-cart. I shall never forget that drive; the warmth of the evening was perfect, not too oppressive, the stars gleamed brilliantly through the feathery trees that overhung the road, and the fire-flies shining like points of electric light danced beside us. At length high up, barring the way as it seemed, seen between the avenue of trees, rose a mighty conical hill overgrown with vegetation and outlined on the blueness of the moonlit sky. It was one of the monuments of a bygone age that we had come to see. We could hardly believe that this was really the work of man's hands and not a natural hill. As it turned out to be almost outside the gates of the rest-house it was the one of all the monuments we grew to know and love the best. Imagine a symmetrical hill between two and three hundred feet high, made of solid brick, and so old that the trees, and grass, and soil have overlaid it like jungle. The form of it is said to be " as a bubble of water resting on a liquid surface." This is the famous Ruanveli dagoba, built by King Dutugemini about B.C. 160, and there, not far from it, lies the uptilted slab of granite on which the dying king was laid so that his closing eyes might light their last on his proudest monument.

It is quite impossible to describe the wonders of this City of Seventy Kings. The best of it is one is free to wander anywhere, there are few European visitors, the place is unspoiled by guides and crowds. The ruins cover acres and acres of ground. There are several dagobas scattered at various distances resembling Ruanveli in form, and most of them have, as it has, a flat causeway of hewn granite blocks, wide enough for six elephants to walk abreast, running round them. Stretches of park-like ground covered with short grass lie near, and in the glorious light of a tropical moon we three linked arms and wandered over the warm turf amid the shadows of the trees ; we were, I must confess, terribly afraid of snakes, but the event justified the risk. We passed on to a smaller dagoba glistening like marble in the moonlight ; this is Thuparama, the oldest of all the monuments. It was built in B.C. 307 to enshrine the right jaw of the Buddha, "which, descending from the skies, placed itself upon the crown of the monarch's head." In spite of this signal relic Thuparama is not so impressive as the others, being so much smaller, more of the type of the ordinary Burmese pagoda; it is coated by chunam, a kind of white cement, and certainly in the moonlight this adds greatly to its charm.

On every side lie fallen or upright columns of granite with carved capitals as fresh as when they were done two thousand years ago. In the daylight we hired the small pony cart which had brought us from the station, and drove from one mighty sight to another, we visited Jetawarana a stupendous pile of masonry clothed, like Ruanveli, with a growth of vegetation, which has here and there broken from its roothold and fallen, showing layers upon layers of red brick; at the summit, still erect in its hoary age, is a pointing finger in the shape of a brickwork tower. The platform around the base of the dagoba is overgrown with trees and bushes, which have burst up between the joints of the stone work, little paths run here and there and among them birds sing sweetly, and butterflies with bodies almost as big as birds flutter gaily in the sunshine. Bits of ruined capitals and other carving lie about half buried in the tangle of rank-growing weeds and bush.

But we did not see only dagobas, we saw also tanks like Roman baths, with steps descending into them, having grey shadows on their carved balustrades, and lying deserted save for a tiny yellow-backed tortoise which walked away with dignity into the grass.

We saw wide reaches of water like inland seas edged with green mounds or bunds, all artificial. We saw one thousand six hundred hewn columns set so thickly that hardly had one room to pass between, these were once the famous Brazen Palace, where nine roofs covered with brazen tiles had towered toward the burning sky. We saw, most wonderful of all, the sacred Bo-tree, grown, so tradition says, from a branch of the sacred Bo-tree under which the Lord Buddha received revelation; brought from India by a princess and planted in B.C. 245, the oldest historical tree in the world, and as the legend says: "always green, never growing or decaying." Whatever its origin, the copious references to it in chronicles of many centuries give it a right to an indisputable claim of over two thousand years of age. It was evening time when we approached. The entrance is by granite steps polished by the bare feet of countless generations, and carved with wonderful figures of elephants and horses in procession round what is called the moonstone, or projecting slab before the actual steps. Outside men sat and sold sweet flowers to be offered in reverence. Arranged in little cardboard saucers, so that they looked like one great blossom, was a central pink lotus with an array of white frangipanni around.

The low wall, black-red with age, that runs around the first court, is guarded by tall growing palms. Up through the broken pavement within, spring many small bo-trees, offspring of the parent stem. Groups of natives sat around gleaming fires which caught the bright fabrics of their dress in weird lights. Up yet

other steps all broken and dilapidated we went, to
another terrace, and then above our heads we saw the
gnarled and crooked branches of the ancient tree.

Very few leaves were there on it, and when one
fluttered down a zealous pilgrim hastened to pick it up
as a precious relic. They are like the leaves of the
balsam-poplar, but the terminal spike is much longer.
The tree is old and straggly without grandeur of size or
proportion, but encompassed about with the reverence of
generations past numbering, and as we stood there over-
shadowed by those hoary branches and drank in all the
weird beauty of the scene, the warm orange light of the
sunset, against which the line of tall palms showed black,
while the monkeys leaped from bough to bough looking
like little black demons; and as the delicate scents of the
floral offerings were wafted around us, and the slow chant
of the devotees came to our ears, something of the awe
and veneration which inspired the worshippers crept into
our hearts. I felt I could not come again next day in
the full blaze of the blatant sunshine, I must always
remember it, always see it, as I saw it then, while the
mystery of the evening deepened around it.

In comparison with this everything else paled in
interest, and it is a fitting end—after a journey amid the
ancient civilisation of peoples to whom our generations
are but as the growth of field grass—to pause beside the
roots of the sacred Bo-tree.

INDEX

2 M

Printed by
BALLANTYNE & CO. LIMITED
Tavistock Street, London

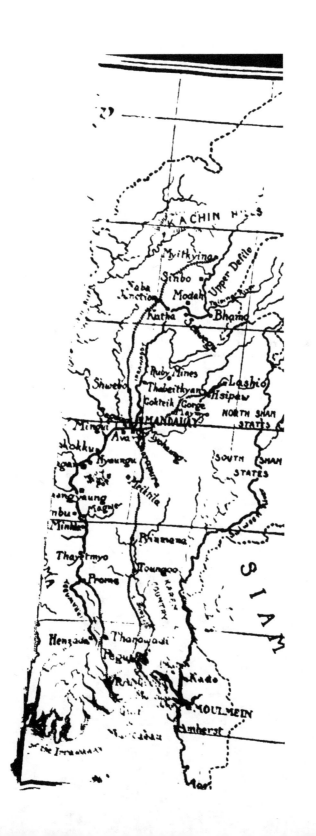

Printed by
BALLANTYNE & CO. LIMITED
Tavistock Street, London

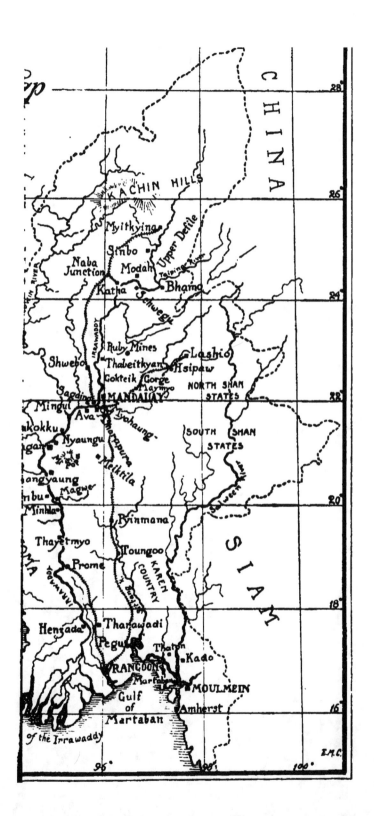

CHINA

KACHIN HILLS

Myitkyina

Sinbo

Naba
Junction   Modah   Upper Defile

Katha   Bhamo

Ruby Mines

Shwebo   Thabeitkyan   Lashio

Gokteik Gorge   Hsipaw

Maymyo   NORTH SHAN

MANDALAY   STATES

Mingui   Ava

akokku   Nyaungu   SOUTH SHAN
STATES

angyaung   Meiktila

Magwe

mbu   Minhla

Pyinmana

Thayetmyo   Toungoo

Prome   KAREN
COUNTRY

Henzada   Tharrawadi

Pegu   Thaton

RANGOON   Kado

Martaban   MOULMEIN

Gulf
of   Amherst

Martaban

of the Irrawaddy

SIAM

E.M.C.